MW01054751

MINIATURE VIGNETTES

MINIATURE VIGNETTES

Susan Rogers Braun

CHARLES SCRIBNER'S SONS

NEW YORK

Copyright © 1975 Susan Rogers Braun

Library of Congress Cataloging in Publication Data

Braun, Susan Rogers.
    Miniature vignettes.

    Includes index.
    1. Miniature objects. 2. Models and modelmaking.
I. Title.
NK8470.B72   745.5   75-11962
ISBN 0-684-14378-X

This book published simultaneously in the
United States of America and in Canada—
Copyright under the Berne Convention

All rights reserved. No part of this book
may be reproduced in any form without the
permission of Charles Scribner's Sons.

1 3 5 7 9 11 13 15 17 19 C/MD 20 18 16 14 12 10 8 6 4 2

Printed in the United States of America

To Bert, David, and Jeff

Contents

Preface

Miniature Vignettes describes for the first time a craft that presents the challenge of miniaturizing within a specific framework—a framework which simultaneously demands the faithful copying of reality and the manipulation of a limited space.

It is this spatial characteristic that distinguishes vignettes from doll houses and miniature rooms. The vignettist must address himself to achieving the perception of great depth where only a token space exists.

This book is intended as a practical guide for the growing number of student vignettists, and for all hobbyists who wish to master the technique of scale reduction in other related art and craft pursuits. Though the vignette concept is an approach to miniatures unique and separate from doll houses and miniature rooms, many of the vignette techniques, both in the stimulation of ideas and practical application, will appeal to such fanciers for the new and added dimensions that may be applied to their work.

In the more than a decade since I have been making miniature vignettes, and in the years since it has been offered as a course of instruction, I have felt for myself and have seen others experience a wide range of satisfactions and new involvements that I, for one, have not found together in any other single craft. This would certainly help .to explain the unusually keen reception miniature vignettes have received in a relatively short exposure to public view, and its rapid growth as a new craft pursuit.

Though miniature vignettes were first introduced as a course of study to a limited number of students at the Willow Brook Art Center in Long Grove, Illinois in 1971, their most important exhibition was at The Beehive Studio in Deerfield, Illinois early in 1972. I was invited by Laura Davis, owner of the studio, to teach this new spatial concept to her découpage and *vue d'optique* students. So enthusiastically were vignettes received that the studio has since converted largely to classes and supplies for miniature craftsmen, both for the individual student and, in seminars, for teachers and dealers across the country.

In the Beehive classes many of the techniques were advanced and refined, and should be credited to Mrs. Davis, and also to staff members Muriel Hoffman and Iova Vaughn. Credit also must be acknowledged to the numerous students who, highly motivated and stimulated in their own individual vignette projects, contributed—and continue to do so—unique improvisations and extension of original ideas. Many of the vignettes illustrated are the work of students tutored by the capable Beehive staff.

Special acknowledgement should be given to Muriel M. Knudsen for her many fine line drawings throughout the book.

On a personal note, I thank my good friends, Warren Rogers and Maryn Johnson, and my husband and two sons, who for many years shared the dining room table with miniature work in process, for their encouragement in the task of bringing *Miniature Vignettes* to print.

Susan Rogers Braun

PART 1
PLANNING

1

Qualities of the Miniature Vignette

A cursory glance at miniature vignettes might seem to show just another stage upon which to work and play with miniatures, a subject that in one form or another has fascinated people since primitive man first fashioned doll-like objects and other miniature playthings of wood and bone.

But a closer look reveals a unique characteristic that separates vignettes from the toys, doll houses, and miniature rooms where life-size objects are reduced in direct proportion to actual size. Height and width in miniature vignettes are accurately reduced, but since the depth of the project is only a fraction of what it would be in life-size scale, artistic tricks and liberties are taken to achieve the perception and sensation of a depth greater than exists. A vignette can be made in many sizes, depending upon the scale chosen for the interior, but its depth should be held to a fractional representation.

In 1″ equals 1′ scale, for instance, the maximum depth should be 6″ or less. Some of the vignettes illustrated are only 2″ to 3″ deep. A vignette more than 5″ deep looks awkward when hung on a wall, though a 6″ project can be displayed gracefully on a shelf or table.

A photograph of a well-executed vignette can deceive the camera and be passed off as the image of a full-sized setting (Photo 1). And though a vignette represents only a token portion—a wall or corner—of a room, at its most accomplished it can project to the viewer a sense that he is encompassed by four walls or by the outdoors.

Like the painter who creates the illusion of depth on a two-dimen-

Photo 1: Oriental Room, Edna Eddy. 8″ x 10″ x 5″. Photo: George Peterson

sional canvas, the vignettist must dip into a bag of trompe l'oeil ("fool the eye") tricks and optical illusions to create "a picture" with three-dimensional devices and artistic chicanery.

Miniature vignettes are a creative venture that takes the craftsman, if not into wholly new artistic tasks, into an endeavor which combines familiar work with new disciplines, innovative use of ordinary materials, and an exciting contest with space and man's perceptions of it.

The undertaking will be for many a first exposure to working in scale, and for others a first-time adventure into a new way of recording what their eyes see, if not a new experience in how to see.

Like the famed dolls' houses, many of them once belonging to queens and princesses and now housed in museums around the world, and like the miniature rooms, such as Mrs. J. Ward Thorne's collections at the Chicago Art Institute and Phoenix Art Gallery and those of miniaturist Eugene Kupjack, miniature vignettes serve to preserve history. They are windows to the past and present, and will take their place as a valued new idiom in recording life styles, customs, and manners of various periods for present and future generations.

The vignette medium, like Colleen Moore's fabled fairy palace in Chicago at the Museum of Science and Industry, proffers an opportunity to revel in the realm of fantasy.

Vignettes are more than mere assemblages of minutiae. They can capture the vignettist's dreams, memories, personal yearnings or visual impressions of the past. They can be a walk into a fairy tale, a literary picture, or a stopped-action look at a moment in history. They can tell a story or evoke a mood.

Clever subtleties, not dolls, suggest human "occupancy" in a vignette—the impression that someone has just walked out of the setting or is about to enter it. A human figure should be included *only* if it

Photo 2: Toy Butcher Stall 1840, Susan Rogers Braun. 9″ x 12″ x 4½″. Photo: Fred Slater

is an essential part of the representational intent, as in the stylized, interpretative version of a toy butcher stall (Photo 2). The artist's aim here was to reproduce in vignette form a toy of 1840 which was played with by a young owner; the detachable meats and movable butcher "doll" are integral elements.

Though vignettes can be created with sophisticated power tools by those with the means, space, and desire to work with such equipment, the ones recommended here have deliberately been restricted to simple hand tools that the novice can use with very little practice anywhere in the home.

No special cabinets or tables are required for display of vignettes, for their overall dimensions permit them to be hung on a wall like a deep shadow box, or placed on a shelf or end table.

Lighting is not necessary in the shallow vignette box, though some vignettists have installed background lighting for special effects.

2

Choosing a Subject

Like a blank canvas on the painter's easel, the raw vignette shell frames an empty space in which the artistic task is to create a "picture," a three-dimensional composition of a setting in miniature that approximates the reality of full-scale life.

The artist should choose a topic or theme with special meaning. This elevates the vignette above a mere fancy display of miniatures or a fractional version of a doll's room.

A good vignette can capture, in frozen motion, an instant of a treasured memory, an historic moment, a fantasy. In a sense it is a time capsule that describes how life is or was or even how the vignettist might like it to be. The more revealing it is of the artist's tastes and interests, the more treasured the vignette is as a gift, a decorative addition to the home, or an heirloom for future generations.

The potential for original subject matter is as varied and limitless as life itself. The problem is not so much "where can I get an idea?" as sifting down to one choice from a wealth of possibilities. For the beginner having difficulty selecting his first theme, it may be helpful to see the various and wide-ranging categories frequently chosen by teachers and students.

Memories and celebrations: Thanksgiving dinner on grandmother's farm, the honeymoon suite, a son's or daughter's graduation dinner, the night before Christmas (Photo 3), the attic window where rainy days were spent as a child, an interesting place one lived in—a foreign country (Photo 4), military base, ranch, farm, bohemian-style Greenwich Village apartment, college dormitory.

Travel: Preparations for a trip abroad, a favorite place such as an

17

Photo 3: 'Twas the Night Before Christmas, Laura Davis, The Beehive Studio. 9″ x 12″ x 5½″. Photo: George Peterson

Photo 4: Italian Harvest, Nanette Barber. 9″ x 12″ x 5¼″. Photo: George Peterson

Photo 5: English Pub, Mrs. Edward J. McArdle. 9″ x 14″ x 6″. Photo: George Peterson

English pub (Photo 5), Italian restaurant, Mexican silver or basket mart, French Quarter in New Orleans, the Williamsburg restorations in Virginia.

Times past: An old-time butcher stall with sawdust on the floor, an ice cream parlor with marble top tables, metal chairs, overhead fan and tall cool sodas, the corner delicatessen with pickles in a barrel, an early country store, a neighborhood bakery, the open stalls of a green grocer, a barber shop with striped pole, a tobacconist's shop (Photo 6), the fishmonger's store, a millinery, an old book store, an early bathroom (Photo 7), an eighteenth-century German kitchen (Photo 8).

Hobbies or special talents: The kitchen of a gourmet cook, a needlepoint shop (Photo 9), a sewing room, a garden shed, an antique shop (Photo 10), collections of mugs, duck decoys, old trains or dolls, hobbies such as boat or airplane models, repairing old clocks, découpage, musical instruments.

Photo 6: Tobacco Shop (London circa 1750), Nanette Barber. 9″ x 12″ x 5¼″.
Photo: George Peterson

Photo 7: An Early Bathroom, Priscilla Billington. 9″ x 10½″ x 5½″. Photo:
George Peterson

Photo 8: Nuremberg Kitchen 1730, Maryn Johnson. 9″ x 12″ x 4½″. Photo: Fred Slater

Photo 9: Needlepoint Shop, Jane Shaheen. 9″ x 12″ x 5″. Photo: George Peterson

Photo 10: Antique Shop, Maryn Johnson. 9″ x 12″ x 4″. Photo: George Peterson

Literary subjects and special interest studies: Memorabilia of Winston Churchill's career or Benjamin Franklin's interests, the paraphernalia of a Sherlock Holmes story, Tom Sawyer's famed whitewashed fence, the tea party in *Alice in Wonderland*.

Professions: An early-day apothecary, a replica of Abe Lincoln's law office, an architect's drafting corner, a chemist's laboratory, carpenter's workshop, politician's campaign headquarters, blacksmith's shop, flower shop (Photo 11).

Raising a family: The nursery, a teenager's room with pop bottles, posters, stuffed animals, and records, a birthday party for Raggedy Ann, a memorable Christmas with decorated tree, packages, and stockings "hung by the chimney with care."

Historical rooms of other periods: Shaker farm house, the room in

Photo 11: Flower Shop, Muriel Hoffman, The Beehive Studio. 9″ x 12″ x 5½″.
Photo: George Peterson

which Betsy Ross stitched the first American flag, an Early American kitchen, a trading post in New Salem, Illinois, a shipping merchant's office, Mary Todd Lincoln's Springfield parlor, an elegant Virginia tobacco planter's sitting room in Colonial times, a Pilgrim cabin, an eighteenth-century French bedroom (Photo 12).

Photo 12: Eighteenth-Century French Bedroom, Virginia Lanham. 9″ x 12″ x 5¼″.
Photo: George Peterson

A PERSONAL TOUCH

The charm of a vignette is further heightened if a cherished item from one's personal life, or one handed down through a family's generations, is incorporated into the design.

It might be a treasured charm from an old bracelet or a miniature salvaged from an early doll house that fits or can be adapted to the proper scale. A scrap of lace from an ancestor's wedding dress or a handerkerchief made by a grandmother or favorite aunt could be fashioned into curtains or a table covering, adding heirloom value to the vignette. A small snapshot with the faces of subjects in tiny scale can be cut apart for framing and displayed on a wall or over a mantel.

An antique brooch can often be made into a handsome Victorian picture frame, or a bead from a string of old crystal, broken and tucked away in the recesses of a jewelry box, may be combined with other findings to become an elegant old-fashioned perfume bottle or decanter.

SUGGESTION OF OCCUPANCY

A vignette should be "brought to life" without the use of dolls, in subtle touches that suggest the existence of occupants and their activities.

Photo 13: Cards Blowing in Breeze, Susan Rogers Braun. 6½″ x 7¼″ x 2¼″. Photo: George Peterson

Photo 14: Fishing Shanty, Susan Rogers Braun. 5″ x 7″ x 2″. Photo: George Peterson

A newspaper can be left open on a lounge chair with slippers and pipe nearby, a playing card may have slipped to the floor from the stack on the table or be seen fluttering in the breeze from an open window (Photo 13). A hunter's boots might be smeared with mud, or flour spilled on the baker's work table. A Christmas morning scene could include discarded gift wrappings and an already broken toy. An apple has a bite out of it, or the scene might include a half-finished needlepoint project or painted canvas. A trap with a piece of cheese hints at mice; a few nuts on a window ledge, a friendly squirrel.

The unseen inhabitant in the fishing shanty (Photo 14) is suggested both by the basket of clams from the day's digging dripping onto a crumpled newspaper, and by "wet" sandy footprints on the floor that testify to recent use. It is easily imagined that a fisherman has just stepped out of the shack.

IMPORTANCE OF RESEARCH

An effort should be made to portray correctly and authentically the period of the chosen subject matter and to avoid inclusion of items not yet invented or in popular use.

Like other art forms, miniature vignettes may later be a means of identifying aspects of human experience as it existed at a given time. The careful vignettist will not violate what can be a factual account of history and life styles.

The research that might be necessary for a particular subject is one of the added dimensions of miniature vignette craftsmanship that offers an opportunity for the artist's own personal expansion. For many of us, the time spent poking through libraries, museums, and antique stores is one of the most satisfying and fun aspects of good vignette making.

A few minutes in the reference stacks turn up the facts that will prevent the vignettist from including an electric light socket with pull chain in a pre-1896 setting, or telephones before they were installed in residences in 1877. Information of this sort is recorded in such resource books as *Famous First Facts* by Joseph Nathan Kane, as well as other data that will aid the vignettist. Its pages also tell, for example, that the patent for the banjo-style clock was issued in 1802, the first American flag was made in 1777, that ice cream sodas were first "demonstrated" in the summer of 1874 in Philadelphia, and that, while bottles were made in Jamestown, Virginia in 1608 before the Pilgrims landed, the first milk bottles were made in 1879 in Cumberland, Maryland.

Another resource, *Antique Toys and Their Background* by Gwen White, informs us that teddy bears were a craze in 1907, a few years after President Theodore Roosevelt granted permission to a toy store proprietor to make and introduce to the market a "Teddy's bear," named after the president for his unwillingness to shoot a bear cub on a hunting trip in 1902.

3

Aids to Plotting Space

The art of miniature vignettes requires an understanding of how we see, and an appreciation of how both optical illusion and artistic license can be utilized to overcome the limitations of the working space, especially depth.

Two techniques will be described later in this chapter to help the vignettist become more accustomed to this spatial restriction and to practice working within it.

OPTICAL ILLUSION

One limitation of visual ability can be made to work to advantage in vignette making—simply that when looking head-on into a scene, the eye is unable to perceive the true depth of objects, and even if the spectator is slightly to one side or higher or lower than the objects being viewed, depth is "seen" in foreshortened lines that are not an accurate discernment of true measurements.

For example, when standing at one end of a room and looking across it, it is not possible to see how deep are the bookshelves, a fireplace, a room beyond an open door, a stairway on the far wall. The pieces of furniture and doorway openings along the side walls seem narrower than their true widths.

Making use of this optical illusion, the vignettist can greatly reduce the depth measurements of furniture, shelving, and other details on the back wall and somewhat on the side walls, to the point where such shortening of lines would look awkward and distorted.

This little trick, executed in such a way as still to preserve realism, allows additional working space for other elements in the vignette.

ARTISTIC LICENSE

Imagine a full-size dining table with chairs in varying scales set around it—a throne, a nursery school seat, an average-sized chair.

This exaggerated image illustrates the importance of adhering to the selected scale. In the limited space of a vignette, one false judgment can destroy the ability that a good vignette should have to fool the camera (and eye) when uniformity of scale and fine craftsmanship are coupled.

Until one's eye is retrained to see and make accurate judgments in the chosen scale, and to recognize instinctively the size relationship of each item to each other item included, measuring is essential. The ruler, then, is an important tool, but contradictorily it is not always the final criterion.

Another factor that comes into play is artistic license that permits, in a few instances, the use of a miniature that measurement alone might reject. In this sense, another "tool" is one's power of observation of the world around us and the ability to perceive that the size of a particular object is not always a constant perception, but can seem larger or smaller by virtue of varying judgment.

Figure 1 demonstrates how one accessory (a candlestick) might be used interchangeably among some scales, while another cannot, depending upon the concept of its size in full scale.

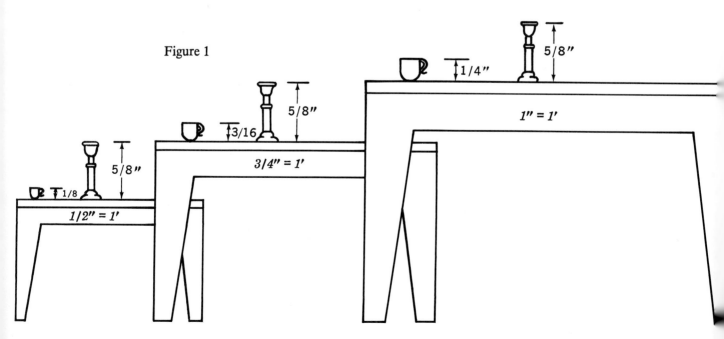

Figure 1

The candlestick illustrated is an example of an accessory that can be used in several scales, while the coffee mug shown is less versatile. The ⅝″ candlestick would be 7½″ high in 1″ scale; a 15″-tall design in ½″ scale; and 10″ high in ¾″ scale. All of these heights are reasonable visual interpretations, for candleholders of this design come in many sizes. The coffee mug depicted is 3″ in life size and in its reductions to ½″, ¾″ and 1″ scales is ⅛″, ³⁄₁₆″, and ¼″ respectively. The ¼″-high mug is too large to be used on the ½″ scale table, though it might be used on the ¾″ scale table. The ⅛″ mug would look too small on the ¾″ and 1″ scale tables. The vignettist should keep in mind that an accessory viewed subjectively in this manner must still have a realistic relationship to other in-scale objects used in the same setting.

PLANNING AIDS

Two devices are suggested as aids in plotting the vignette and working effectively in its height, width, and depth.

The first of these is a rough sketch of the proposed basic ideas on a sheet of paper the same size as the shell opening. It is especially helpful to work on graph paper, two pages taped together if necessary.

This is a two-dimensional plan that begins the composition of the finished three-dimensional picture. Such a sketch need not be very competent artwork to help in the recognition and understanding of the restricted space.

The other device is a technique demonstrating the working space of the third dimension, depth, as well as continuing to assist in height and width considerations. Working within the chosen shell, you can make a cardboard mockup of the picture plan. Create simple models of furniture and special effects, cut out of cardboard and roughly assembled into basic shapes with glue and pins and held temporarily in place with masking tape or mounting adhesive. If miniatures have already been acquired for the project, you can use them instead.

The roughest of sketches and the most rudimentary cardboard models will pose the spatial problems to be addressed by the vignettist in the initial planning, and will illustrate the need to "compose" the content much as an artist composes a drawing to achieve good balance of line and mass.

COMPOSITIONAL GUIDELINES

Good composition obtains if the techniques of arrangement used by artists, photographers, and interior decorators are employed. We use many of these principles in the everyday experiences of arranging furniture, making a centerpiece, landscaping a garden, accessorizing a dress, hanging pictures, or arranging objects in a curio cabinet.

Effects that divide the box in half, either horizontally or vertically, such as placing a wall molding in a horizontal line running midway from top to bottom, or putting a column dead center, should be avoided. The planes formed by table tops, cabinet pieces, shelving and other effects, if all falling on the same level, tend to produce monotony.

A more eye-pleasing effect is achieved if clusters of items are executed in odd, rather than even, numbers. Use three, five, or seven flowers in a vase instead of two, four, or six.

Allow for some "free," unused space in the composition. If the vignette is crammed full of miniatures, it will not only appear cluttered, perhaps even eye-tiring, but will also make it difficult for the viewer to appreciate the fine points of workmanship and the story the vignettist wants to suggest. The advertising layout artist utilizes the principle that unfilled space can be a dominant and important element in directing the viewer's eye to the message.

Edit out some accessories if too many are planned. While certain subjects allow for a feeling of clutter—a second-hand shop, attic, antique store—*real* clutter should not exist. Objects can be overlapped and grouped, which also assists in achieving a sense of depth. Furniture should not all be lined up flat along the walls. The slightest angling of a chair, for instance, provides a slanted line or plane that helps to convey the feeling of depth. If too much furniture has been planned, it is better to eliminate a piece and save it for the next project than to crowd it in.

Walls, and sometimes ceilings, can be slanted in many plans to help create the illusion of depth. Other three-dimensional devices are wall alcoves, built-in cupboards, ceiling beams, corner cupboards or a door standing ajar.

Another important spatial consideration, and one of the most effective for creating a sense of depth, is the proper selection and placement of a background print. This will be discussed in the next chapter.

4

Selecting a
Background Print

The miniature vignette concept presents the intriguing challenge of creating the impression of depth many times greater than the actual working space.

Though a vignette represents merely a fraction of a full-size room, it is the artistic goal to make the viewer feel he is *in* the room.

All the artifice possible should be employed to accomplish the illusion of depth. Devices such as doors opening into another room, stairways, fireplaces, and walls with a projection or offset aid in this objective, as does the shortening of some depth measurements (discussed in Chapter Three).

But one of the most effective techniques for manipulating depth sensations in a trompe l'oeil manner is the inclusion of a background print, seen through windows and doors, that not only introduces the impression of distance (Photo 15) but also involves the viewer in the world outside the vignette, and in many instances adds information to establish location and historical period.

The outdoor background might be a scene that shows a view "as far as the eye can see," or one that simply illustrates the street and buildings across the road or a garden wall and foliage.

In selecting a print, all of the following points should be considered: the scale of objects shown, the perspective, placement, eye level, size, and color compatibility with the vignette interior.

Photo 15: The Greenhouse, Pam Nellis. 9″ x 12″ x 4″. Photo: George Peterson

SCALE

A print with objects that are in a scale larger than that used in the vignette obviously is not suitable, for objects appear smaller the farther away they are.

Elements in the foreground, such as a tree trunk, fence, or people, can be in the same scale as the interior.

If everything pictured in the print is of much smaller scale than the interior, the question must be asked if this smaller scale is too abrupt a change from the interior one.

Color photography by George Peterson

Early Shipping Merchant's Office, Susan Rogers Braun. 9″ x 12″ x 2¼″.

Needlepoint Shop, Jane Shaheen. 9″ x 12″ x 5″.

Braunhall, Susan Rogers Braun. 9″ x 12″ x 4½″.

Oriental Room, Edna Eddy. 8″ x 10″ x 5″.

Italian Harvest, Nanette Barber. 9″ x 12″ x 5¼″.

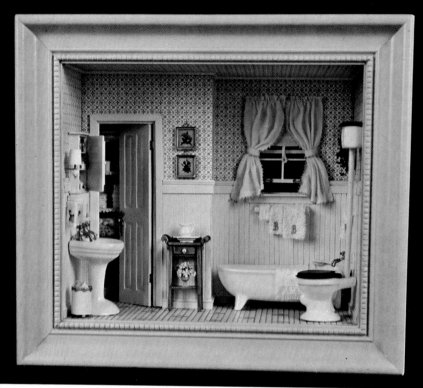

An Early Bathroom, Priscilla Billington. 9″ x 10½″ x 5½″.

The Greenhouse, Pam Nellis. 9″ x 12″ x 4″.

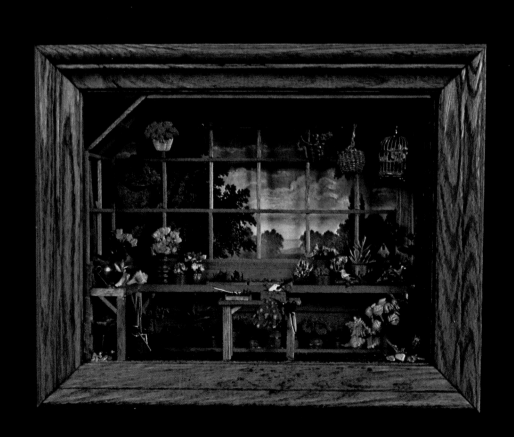

Victorian Boudoir, Susan Rogers Braun. 6½″ x 8½″ x 2¼″.

The Flower Shop, Muriel Hoffman, The Beehive Studio. 9″ x 12″ x 5½″.

Tobacco Shop (London circa 1750), Nanette Barber. 9″ x 12″ x 5¼″.

Antique Shop, Maryn Johnson. 9″ x 12″ x 4″.

'Twas the Night Before Christmas, Laura Davis, The Beehive Studio.
9″ x 12″ x 5½″.

Music Room, Susan Rogers Braun.
6½" x 8½" x 2¼".

Cards Blowing in Breeze, Susan
Rogers Braun. 6½" x 7¼" x 2¼".

Ideally a background view will show objects in the foreground in a scale the same or slightly smaller than in the vignette, with elements of the middle ground appearing smaller and those in the far background smaller still.

PERSPECTIVE

It is a familiar example of optical illusion that railroad tracks seem to join at the horizon line, where the sky and earth appear to meet. The spot where the tracks seem to converge is called the vanishing point.

The selection of a print that utilizes this phenomenon helps to compensate for the actual depth limitation by incorporating into the vignette a visual sensation of looking beyond the setting to a point some distance away. However, the print should not portray the perspective in an exaggerated manner that causes the relationship between the vignette interior and the background scene to appear contrived or distorted.

PLACEMENT

The positioning of a print requires analyzing its content as interpreted by the artist and locating the horizon line. The best level for the horizon can be found by sliding the print up and down within the shell until the perspective is found that most effectively relates to the interior plan.

The background print in the early farm house (Photo 16) shows a woman approaching along a winding pathway, with buildings off in the distance. Not only do the small size of the distant buildings and the flow of the path establish good perspective, but the added artificial corn "growing" immediately outside the window, in the same scale as the interior, provides a foreground that was lacking in the print.

If the horizon line had been placed in a lower position, the woman would have appeared closer, in fact right outside the window, and would have been too small for the interior scale.

EYE LEVEL

Another consideration in print selection is the intended eye level of the viewer "in" the vignette.

Photo 16: Early Farm House, Susan Rogers Braun. 8″ x 10″ x 3¼″. Photo: Fred Slater

Is the vignette interior on ground level? Or is it a second story room or a room in a house atop a hill with a wide-ranging panoramic view? Is the spectator in a basement apartment looking up to street level?

The viewer of the music room (Photo 17) looks out *over* a harbor.

The rooftop of the building immediately below in the print foreground is below the viewer's eye level and informs him that the room is in a building on a hill high above the harbor.

Photo 17: Music Room, Susan Rogers Braun. 6½″ x 8½″ x 2¼″. Photo: George Peterson

SIZE OF PRINT

The reality of a setting is certainly destroyed if the viewer can peek sideways through a window and see the sky coming to an end!

It is not always easy to find a print that will fit exactly in the appropriate position on the back of the vignette shell and still have its edges extend far enough in all directions from windows and doors that they are not visible if the box is tipped or viewed at an angle.

If a print is too small, compensating measures can be taken. One method is to obstruct the viewer's line of sight by adding a protruding exterior wall or edge of an adjacent building, as seen for example through the right window of the music room (Photo 17); or exterior beams, foliage, or any other effect that seems natural outside the door or window can be added. Such additions should coordinate in color and feeling with both the print and the vignette interior.

Or, the print can be enlarged by painting in an extension of its features—the sky, landscape, buildings. This does not require skilled artwork in most cases. Often, just the stippling or sponging on of paint in an appropriate color will suffice, covering the edges of the print and any part of the box surface that is visible.

If working with a large print, it may be possible to cut out sections that would have been discarded and to glue them in as extensions, thereby keeping color and texture coordinated in the background scene.

OTHER BACKGROUNDS

A vignettist with painting experience may choose to paint in the desired background scene himself. Some subjects lend themselves to "construction" of a background in place of a print—for example, fashioning buildings across the street of cardboard and wood facades.

The technique of *vue d'optique* can be employed to create a three-dimensional or raised relief background. The same elements of three or more identical prints are cut out, contoured and then reassembled in slightly separated layers with dabs of silicone seal or balsa wood glued in between them.

WHERE TO FIND PRINTS

Prints may be found in art stores, découpage studios, and many craft shops. Large calendars often provide suitable scenes. A search through old books and magazines may produce the needed background, or landscapes on large Christmas cards occasionally work out well. Scenes reproduced on cardboard to simulate canvas painting, found wherever inexpensive art work is sold, can be used provided the vignette plan does not require the background to bend around a corner. Reproductions of certain Currier and Ives prints are an excellent source of sky and landscape effects and period subjects.

5

Working in Scale

Life-size measurements of objects planned for a vignette must be converted to a uniformly reduced size that will fit into the allotted space.

The scale chosen should be followed faithfully so that the finished vignette will accurately resemble true-to-life relationships.

The easiest scale for the beginner is:

$$1'' = 1'$$

This simply means that one inch in miniature represents one foot in life size.

A formula is given later in the chapter for vignettists wishing to make conversions of full-size dimensions to work in other than $1''$ scale.

One of the reasons that $1''$ scale is suggested for the beginner is that the majority of miniatures on the market are in this scale and they often may be altered or worked directly into a project.

Also, the needed reductions for $1''$ scale are figured handily on an ordinary ruler, and usually are simple enough to calculate mentally.

Each inch on the ruler represents one foot in life size. Six feet in real life is $6''$ on the ruler. A lamp $18''$ high (that is, $1\frac{1}{2}'$) is $1\frac{1}{2}''$ in miniature.

If a fireplace to be copied from real life has a mantel $4'$ from the floor, it would be constructed so the mantel in miniature is $4''$ from the floor line. A $3''$ wide table in minature represents $3'$ in full size.

FRACTIONS

Fractions seem trickier, but need not be a problem.

Since $6''$ in real life is $\frac{1}{2}'$, it would be $\frac{1}{2}''$ in miniature. But how many inches, or fractions of an inch, in real life is ¼″ or ¹⁄₁₆″? Fractions will be less confusing if you keep in mind that:

1″ (miniature) is 1′ or 12″ (life size).

Therefore, a real-life measurement of less than 12″ is expressed as

---

Most Frequently Used Fractions

Scale: 1″ = 1′

		MINIATURE (RULER SIZE)		LIFE SIZE
		1/32″		3/8″
2/32″	or	1/16″		3/4″
		3/32″		1 1/8″
2/16″	or	1/8″		1 1/2″
6/32″	or	3/16″		2 1/4″
4/16″	or	1/4″		3″
8/16″	or	1/2″		6″
6/8″	or	3/4″		9″
		1″		12″

---

a fraction, or so many parts of a 12″ foot. Nine inches in life size is ⁹⁄₁₂ths of a foot or ¾″. Four inches life size is ⁴⁄₁₂ths of a foot or ⅓″. Two inches life size is ²⁄₁₂ths of a foot or ⅙″. If the miniature measure is given as ¼″, it should be interpreted in 1″ scale as meaning one-quarter of a life-size foot or one-quarter of 12″. Therefore one-quarter of a foot is 3″ in real life. A miniature measurement of ¾″ would convert to ¾ of 12″, or 9″.

The listing of Most Frequently Used Fractions, especially for ordering wood supplies, can be used as a conversion guide to save time, but when it is not handy or figures needed are not shown, you will want to be able to make the necessary calculations and should study the formula given in this chapter for working in other scales. It can be used for 1″ scale work, too.

USING A YARDSTICK

Where are the needed life-size measurements to be found?
In designing furniture, the dimensions often are found in resource

books, magazines, and furniture catalogs. Some books dealing with period rooms will give ceiling heights and dimensions of other architectural details.

But for contemporary measures, real-life dimensions can be recorded from actual objects with a ruler or yardstick, and by careful and repeated observation. The same is true of measurements for such detailing as a certain style doorway, window area, and molding dimensions. If a chair rail is to be included, you can note the height of one at home, in a friend's house, or in a department store model room. It usually is 30″ from the floor, or 2½″ in miniature. Most chair seats are 18″ (1½′) from the floor; this fact is gleaned by observing and measuring several chairs.

The yardstick can be used to measure how high door knobs are from the floor, the distance between the ceiling and top of a door molding, the width of baseboards, the size of window panes.

VISUAL JUDGMENTS

The scale of furniture and architectural detailing in various period subjects sometimes varies from contemporary measurements. If actual dimensions cannot be found from books and museums, it is often possible to estimate them by looking at pictures of room settings of that period and comparing visually the size of the piece in question to other given or known data, such as the height of a fireside chair or the typical height from floor to ceiling in a room of that period and style. These visual comparisons of relationships within the picture can be helpful guidelines in scaling furniture and background details.

In most contemporary homes, a ceiling is about 8′ from the floor. While 8″ would be the accurate conversion for ceiling height in a vignette of 1″ scale, the installation of ceiling and floor often requires an allowance of additional space. An added half-inch or so will also keep the composition open and unsqueezed.

Additional inches of height must be allowed for special effects such as a slanted ceiling, a loft, an overhead sign on a store exterior.

With practice, a miniature item held into the vignette shell will easily be seen to be too large, too small, or just right. One miniature can be placed next to another in the proper scale to visually test their relationship. Does a vase "take over" the table; could a properly scaled imaginary person sitting in a chair get his legs under the table? With experience, an out-of-scale miniature will immediately stand out.

SHOPPING IN ONE-INCH SCALE

The 6″ ruler performs in two important ways. It is needed for taking measurements inside the vignette shell, since a larger one will not fit, and it is a convenient size to carry in pocket or purse to make an accurate check of scale when shopping for miniatures.

OTHER SCALES

If working in a scale other than 1″ equals 1′, or when 1″ scale reductions are in fractions or not easily calculated mentally, conversion of life-size measurements to miniature size and conversely, miniature dimensions to life size, are found by substituting known data in the algebraic statement:

$$\frac{a}{b} = \frac{c}{d}$$

The meaning of this statement of relationships for the purpose of vignette making can be written:

$$\frac{a\ (inches\ in\ miniature)}{b\ (feet\ in\ real\ life)} = \frac{c\ (inches\ in\ miniature)}{d\ (feet\ in\ real\ life)}$$

Let a/b represent the scale chosen—such as ½″ equals 1′; ¾″ equals 1′; 1¼″ equals 1′ and so on.

To illustrate in ¾″ scale:

Substitute for symbols a and b:

$$\frac{¾″}{1′} = \frac{c}{d}$$

The data for either c or d must be known. If d (feet in real life) is known, then c (inches in miniature) is the unknown, and conversely.

The height of a table in life size is 3′. How high is it in ¾″ scale?

$$\frac{¾″}{1′} = \frac{c\ (inches\ in\ miniature)}{3′}$$

After substituting known information, cross multiply:

a multiplied by d equals b multiplied by c

Thus: ¾ times 3 = 1 times c

9/4 = 1 c

2¼ = c

Since c represents inches in miniature, the answer is: the table is 2¼ʺ in miniature. If c is the known data, the proper substitution is made, the multiplication followed, and the answer is d (in feet).

> IMPORTANT: In the formula *miniature dimensions are always in inches; real-life dimensions are always in feet.*

Since the relationship of inches to feet must be kept constant, the dimensions of substituted data must be consistent.

If, for instance, the real life dimension, always expressed in feet, is given as 18ʺ, it must be changed to 1½′. If the life-size measurement is less than a foot, it must be changed to its fractional equivalent in feet: for example, 3ʺ life size would be expressed in the formula as ³⁄₁₂ths or ¼′.

If the miniature measure is shown as a half foot, it should be changed to 6ʺ.

PART 2
MECHANICS

6

Tools, Supplies, and their Sources

Here is a list of the basic tools and supplies used in most vignette construction, followed by a list of other helpful tools and supplies which may occasionally be needed.

The way the tools are used is described, along with suggestions on likely sources for finding them, and some helpful tips for working with them.

Basic Tools

craft knife with straight-edge blade and pointed tip
razor saw
razor blade, single edge, in holder
12″ metal ruler with nonslip backing
6″ ruler
sharp pencils

Basic Supplies

balsa wood and/or basswood
illustration board ⅛″ thick
wood stains
acrylic and/or oil paints
brushes or foam rubber sponge
glass or masonite cutting board
white resin glue
clear contact cement

hinges and/or screw eyes and screws
saw-toothed hanger

For shell and frame preparation:
vignette shell
frame and glass
paints or wood stains
white shellac
denatured alcohol
varnish, eggshell or satin finish
turpentine
silicone seal, if desired
beige sandpaper, #220 or medium coarse
black wet-dry sandpaper, #600 or extra fine
tack rag

Other Helpful Tools

needle files
scissors
pliers
tweezers
awl or ice pick
wire cutter
small screwdriver
small miter box
emery board

Other Optional Supplies

background print, if used
graph paper, 4 or 8 squares to the inch for 1″ scale work
modeling compound
fabrics with in-scale designs
paper with in-scale designs
clear acrylic spray
glue for fabric
reusable mounting adhesive
spray varnish
enamel model paints
tiny paint brushes
small wood moldings

gold paper braids
lightweight cardboard
clear epoxy glue
wood fill
Spackle
gesso
jewelry parts

The tools for vignette construction are easy to find and use. All required cutting and sawing, using the materials recommended here, can be done with the following tools, all found in craft, art, and hobby outlets: craft knife with straight-edge blade and pointed tip, razor saw, and single-edge razor blade in holder (Photos 18, 19, and 20).

Photo 18: Craft Knife. Photo: Fred Slater

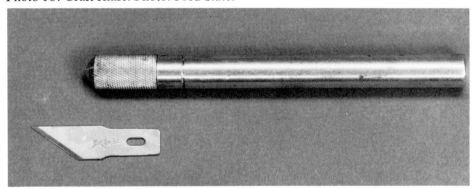

Photo 19: Razor Saw. Photo: Fred Slater

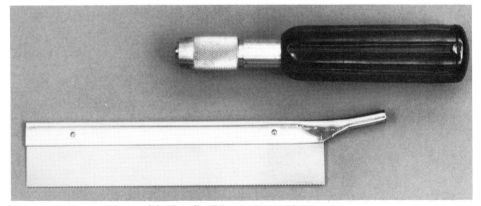

Photo 20: Razor Blade with Handle. Photo: Fred Slater

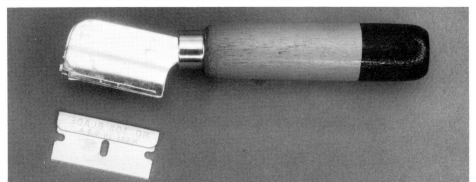

The best woods to use are:

balsa—a soft, lightweight wood with heavy graining, found in hobby and craft stores, familiar for its popular use in airplane and miniature car modeling. It comes in many widths and thicknesses, and can be cut easily in under ½ʺ thickness with a craft knife. Some hobbyists prefer using a razor blade. Use the razor saw for ½ʺ thickness or more.

basswood—a harder and stronger wood than balsa, with a finer grain that gives more finished results. It is not as widely available as balsa, but where it is, it may be purchased in varying widths and thicknesses. It is cut handily with the razor saw. The craft knife can be used on the thinnest pieces and to start sawing lines on thick pieces.

For wall construction, ceilings, floors, and many special effects, use:

illustration board—a smooth-surfaced laminated cardboard approximately ⅛ʺ thick, found in art stores. Cut it with the craft knife or razor blade in a holder.

HANDLING TIPS

The following suggestions for working with these tools and materials are important for both good results and safety:

Balsa and basswood: You should be conscious of the position of your body and hands when using the craft knife or razor blade, keeping fingers out of the way and positioning the body to one side. The knife blade and razor blade should be changed frequently, for a sharp blade gives best results and is safer than a dull one.

The knife should be held in a nearly perpendicular position to the wood when using the tip, or at an angle like a pencil when using the flat edge. Avoid motion that will squeeze and pinch balsa wood, which is extremely soft and pulpy. Guide the side of the blade along a non-slip straight edge, preferably one of metal or a material whose edge will not be shaved with poor cutting and result in irregular lines in later use.

The cutting line should first be scored with two or three firm strokes of the blade tip. Then draw the straight edge of the blade firmly along the scored line until the wood is cut through. On thick pieces of balsa and basswood, use the razor saw by repeatedly drawing it in one direction—toward you.

Curved and carved edges are easier to cut along the grain. Do one small area and remove the waste section by section rather than try to cut the entire sculptured line in one operation. Curlicues cannot be cut from thick basswood with these tools, although from rough cutting the fine shaping can be accomplished by filing. Thin basswood, which can be cut more easily into curved designs, can be laminated to thicker straight pieces of wood or to illustration board.

The wood should be sanded, with the grain, to help reduce graininess. Sand before cutting and then give the cut pieces a light touchup sanding, especially along the edges. Staining should be done before gluing whenever feasible, since stain will not penetrate the glue. If gluing must be done first, unstained spots can be covered up with antiquing.

Thin wood, such as $\frac{1}{32}''$ thick, can be laminated to a curved surface and should be glued on with the graining running up and down. This technique is used when furniture and rounded corner cupboards have been made of cardboard forms and a wood grain surface is desired.

Shellac, varnish, or a spray finish on stained balsa and basswood changes the dull flat surface to a finished glossy one. Two or more coats are usually desired.

Illustration board: The same warning about positioning the body to one side while cutting wood with the craft knife and razor blade applies to illustration board. Sharp blades and the nonslip cutting edge used as a guide are essential for good results and safety.

Score the illustration board deeply two or three times with firm strokes. When almost through the board, one hard cut with the straight edge of the blade may separate the pieces, or the blade tip can be pushed all the way through at the starting end of the scored line and deep cuts made a half inch at a time. If one or two areas still bind while cutting through the layers, raise the board from the work surface and cut through with the tip of the blade. Edges that turn out slanted when they should be straight can be trimmed with the blade or cut with a large sharp scissors if the pieces are small. When a slanted edge is desired, hold the blade in an angled position while cutting. A little practice may be necessary. Feathery edges from imperfect cutting can be improved by sanding with sandpaper or an emery board.

When cutting already small pieces into even smaller ones, fasten them to the cutting board with masking tape to make handling easier and to prevent the work and blade from slipping.

OTHER TOOLS, SUPPLIES

In addition to the 12″ metal ruler with nonslip backing that does double duty as a straight cutting edge, a 6″ ruler is handy for making interior measurements within the shell and can be carried when shopping for miniatures to make on-the-spot measurements.

A constant supply of sharpened pencils is important, for a thick pencil line will throw off measurements in cutting for miniature scale.

A portable cutting surface may be made with a piece of thick glass, about 9″ by 12″. If you place it on corrugated cardboard with the edges covered with masking tape, it is safer to handle and less likely to break when moved about. An additional aid, for quick measurements and cutting, is to place a sheet of graph paper between the glass and its backing. An alternate choice for a cutting surface is a piece of masonite.

Any of the white resin glues that dry clear may be used in all except a few gluing tasks.

Any wood stains and varnishes may be used, following label instructions for procedure and drying times. These directions can vary from one manufacturer's product to another.

Spray varnish, available at hardware stores and some craft shops, is excellent for small, quick jobs such as putting a fast drying finish on tiny moldings and trims or delicate pieces which might break in the normal procedure of brushing or sponging on regular varnish.

The water-base premixed acrylic paints, sold in découpage, hobby, and craft stores, are a preferred choice for their easy clean-up with water, fast drying properties, and wide palette of interesting colors. Oil paints may be used, too, but their 24-hour drying time between coats can mean frustrating delays in a project.

A small piece of foam rubber sponge to wipe on paints, stains, and varnish, thrown away after each use, avoids messy brush clean-ups. An inexpensive foam rubber kneeling pad, found in hardware and discount stores, offers an unlimited supply.

Enamels used for model painting are useful in decorating many accessories and special effects when a glossy surface is desired on plastic, metal, and wood objects. They are found wherever model kits are sold. As they usually come in small jars with tiny openings and are most likely to be used for fine detail work and intricate contoured surfaces, tiny inexpensive brushes should be used. Many plastics and metals, as well as wood, can be painted with acrylic paints provided the items are not handled excessively afterwards. When used on non-porous surfaces, acrylic paint is easily scratched and marred.

Clear contact cement, such as jewelry, household, or craft cement, is recommended when fastening lightweight metals to each other or to wood. Heavier metal items to be joined to each other or to wood may require clear epoxy cement. Both types are available at hobby and hardware stores.

The hardware chosen for fastening the frame and shell should permit reopening the vignette if necessary later. If hinges are preferred, usually two small hinges or one long piano-style hinge are used with a hasp or small trunk closure on the opposite side. The shape and size of hinge will depend upon the flat working space available on the back of the frame. Hinging may be done from side to side or from top to bottom.

Or, you can fasten the shell and frame together with screw eyes and screws. Hold the frame, with glass included, onto the shell and mark off a spot on the left and right sides where the back edge of the frame lines up on the shell. Remove the frame and put in a screw eye on each side so that the eye opening will be flat against the frame. Insert screws that have heads larger than the eye openings through each eye into the frame. If the vignette is to be hung on a wall, screw a saw-toothed hanger to the top and center of the back of the shell. All the hardware can be found in craft and hardware stores.

Graph paper is an aid to making in-scale drawings of an interior plan and in furniture patterning. The vignettist working in one-inch scale should get paper with four or eight squares per linear inch. It is also available in other scales and can be found at office supply houses, school supply counters, and some art stores.

Many accessories and special effects can be created with modeling compounds, the most desirable of which is a type that is soft while being sculpted and manipulated and then is baked to permanent hardness in a moderately heated oven in about 15 minutes. It can be sawed, carved on, drilled, painted. Craft stores are the best source.

Patterned fabrics and papers to be used as wall coverings and fabrics for upholstering furniture should have tiny stripes and motifs that are in scale. They may be ordered from sources that carry supplies for miniaturists but diligent searching often produces results close to home. Sometimes you can find appropriate fabrics at large fabric stores and in such unlikely places as a lined garment or purse, or men's ties about to be discarded.

Papers with in-scale patterns can be found now and then in gift wrap departments and wallpaper books from companies that specialize in mini-prints. They may be ordered, too, from sources that carry supplies for doll houses and miniature rooms. Papers that are exceedingly thin present problems in smooth gluing, but occasionally can be used if first sprayed with clear acrylic sealer two or three times on both sides.

Clear acrylic spray, found in découpage, craft, and art stores, is applied to the back of fabrics three to four times to prevent glue from soaking through to the right side. For fabric work, use a glue made especially for fabrics. It is available at many craft stores. As fabric contents vary, it is a good idea to test them beforehand.

Reusable mounting adhesive, the type that is activated by stretching for a moment between the fingers, is helpful for temporarily holding into place unglued walls, furniture, and accessories during the checking out of installation and composition. Office supply houses, découpage, craft, and hobby shops carry it.

Lightweight cardboard, such as poster board and shirt cardboard, is not sturdy enough for back wall construction when it is set forward from the back of the shell or for angled walls; but is often used for side walls, floor, and ceiling effects that are applied flat against the shell. It can be laminated when thicker cardboard is needed. Art stores and school supply counters stock it.

Decorative wood moldings in small scale are used for baseboards, chair rails, and other wall, ceiling, and furniture trims. They are not easily obtained in all areas, but can be ordered from firms that carry wood specialties and from miniature suppliers. You can design your own moldings by combining a variety of narrow strips of balsa or basswood, or simulate them by painting the raised-relief gold paper braids and bandings that are found at découpage shops and craft centers.

A small miter box, with 45-degree angles, is an optional tool. It is an aid in window construction, picture-frame making, and angling decorative wood moldings and baseboards to fit neatly into corners; however, many vignettists with a little practice can accomplish a mitered cut by eye to very acceptable standards. Small miter boxes are usually found in hobby, and some hardware and craft stores.

Wood fill, found in paint and hardware stores, may be used if repairs are necessary for gouges or holes in wood. Spackle, also available at paint and hardware stores, is used as mortar for stone fireplaces.

Gesso, from art stores, may be used for the effect of plastered walls or when gold paper braids and motifs are combined with a background and need to be integrated for a carved look. Acrylic paints achieve the same result.

Jewelry parts, often used to create raised-relief designs and to fashion many accessories, can be purchased at stores specializing in jewelry-making supplies and at many craft stores, but also can be reclaimed from cast-off or broken jewelry.

7

Choosing and Preparing Shell and Frame

The first step in a vignette project is the selection and preparation of shell and frame.

For appearance and durability, wood shells are preferred over cardboard shells, which may warp, damage easily, and present problems in framing and hanging.

When this author created her first vignettes, deep boxes with proper size openings were unobtainable at craft shops, so the first vignettes were made in large wood cigar boxes or corrugated cardboard shells. Though ceilings, floors, and walls helped to reinforce the cardboard shells, some of these early models have proved to be extremely fragile and require special packing when moved. They are difficult to frame and hang, and in most instances the glass had to be permanently glued to the shell.

Craft centers now stock boxes with dimensions suitable for vignettes. In areas where they cannot be found, the vignettist should make one or find a willing carpenter to put together a shell that best fits the size and scale of the planned project.

Any wood, usually ¼″ thick to avoid warping, can be used, although the choice should take into account that the shell should be finished as a handsome addition to household decor. It is not necessary to use hard woods, for soft woods, like basswood and pine, are in fact easier to sand and to fasten on hardware and hinges without a drill. A shell constructed of good plywood can prove to be quite satisfactory.

A vignette can be created in any size box that relates to the scale chosen for the interior, but the ideal shell for the beginning vignettist working in 1″ equals 1′ scale is a 9″ x 12″ box with a depth less than 6″. If ¼″ stock is used, the frontal opening will be 8½″ x 11½″.

Ceiling heights may vary according to the subject matter, but 8½″ provides the proper space to represent the usual height of a full-size room with an allowance for the thickness of separate ceiling and floor units and to avoid a compressed-looking interior. The 11½″ width affords a good proportion to the height for the sense of a full-scale room; however, this dimension can be varied depending on how much or how little of the setting is to be portrayed. The frame for a 9″ by 12″ box is easily obtained from standard stock at art and craft stores so that a custom-size frame need not be ordered.

The shell may be used vertically, with 11½″ being the height, when a plan calls for special ceiling effects.

A shell deeper than 5″ looks awkward when framed and hung, though a slightly deeper box can be displayed on a shelf or in a bookcase. A shallow box limits more severely the furnishings and effects that may be incorporated, but increases the challenge of achieving the impression of greater depth. Some of the vignettes illustrated here are only two to three inches deep.

Deep shadow boxes whose dimensions are suitable for vignettes sometimes come with fitted frames. Otherwise you can buy a frame in an art, craft, or framing shop. If one cannot be found to fit the shell from standard stock sizes, a custom-made frame can be ordered to specifications, taking care if a prefinished molding is selected that it is compatible with the colors, subject matter, and period of the vignette interior. It is a good idea to take the shell with you to assure a good fit. You will need to select a frame that has a flat area on the back to which hardware that fastens it to the shell can be mounted.

PREPARATION

If the shell and frame are to match, you should work on them simultaneously with the same paints or stains. The shell must always be completed before interior construction begins, as it is difficult to handle staining, painting, and varnishing later without damaging interior work.

You should keep the interior treatment in mind when choosing the finish for the shell and frame so that the color scheme can be coordinated, and the stains or paints used outside will complement those used inside. The final result should be one of "setting off" the interior without being a distracting or competing influence. If the vignette is to be displayed in a particular location, the colors and wood finishes in that room might be considered.

Good workmanship in finishing the frame and shell will guarantee that the vignette will be a fine addition to the home as well as a valued collector's item. The back of the frame and the outside back of the shell, though usually not on view, should be finished, not only for the satisfaction of superior craftsmanship but also so there are no raw surfaces that later may warp.

STAINING

The shell should be sanded lightly with medium sandpaper along the grain of the wood. If the interior walls are to be painted, you should sand them now. Apply stain by brush or wipe it on with disposable foam rubber sponge. A few light strokes of extra fine, wet-dry sandpaper, used dry while the stain is wet, will help push the stain into the wood more uniformly and reduce the fuzzing of the wood.

After the stain is dry, apply a coat of sealer made up of equal parts of white shellac and denatured alcohol. Wipe or brush it on in one direction only and allow it to dry 30 minutes. The sealer should also be applied to the inside of the shell so the interior wood is treated against warping.

PAINTING

Sand the shell lightly with medium sandpaper along the grain of the wood. Do the interior, too, if the walls are to be painted. A sealer of equal parts of white shellac and denatured alcohol, wiped or brushed on in one direction and allowed to dry 30 minutes, should be applied to the entire shell, inside and outside.

Use three or more thin coats of paint, following manufacturer's instructions for the type of paint chosen. After the first coat of paint, sand lightly with extra fine sandpaper. If water-base acrylic paint is used, the sandpaper should be used dry.

VARNISHING

The satin or eggshell type of varnish is usually preferred over high gloss. Stir it before each use. Three coats provide a good finish. A tack rag, purchased at hardware and paint stores, should be lightly wiped over the surfaces before each varnishing to remove minute dust particles. The drying time between coats is at least 24 hours. Before the final varnish coat, sand the project lightly, just a couple of times back and forth, with *wet* extra fine wet-dry sandpaper.

GLASS IN FRAME

If the glass is to be permanently installed, you can glue it in with clear craft glue or silicone seal. Avoid excessive amounts that might ooze out onto the window area of the glass. Glazing points cannot be used as they will be visible and interfere with fastening the frame to the shell. Many vignettists do not glue in the glass to allow for easier replacement if it is broken and for easy removal for picture-taking without reflection. When the frame and shell are fastened properly, the loose glass presents no problem.

FASTENING FRAME AND SHELL

Do not fasten the frame to the shell until the vignette interior is completed. It is the final step in the vignette project. Methods of fastening are described in Chapter Six.

8

Constructing Special Effects

This chapter is devoted to techniques for the construction of the main special effects in miniature vignettes—walls, windows, doors, floors, ceilings, fireplaces, brick, cobblestone, shingles, wrought iron, designs in relief, and other architectural detailing.

WALLS

Free-standing walls, a main wall set forward from a background print, a shop front, angled walls, and walls with special features that aid in the projection of depth—such as alcoves and stairways (Figure 2) —should be constructed of ⅛″-thick illustration board.

Thick woods might be used, but illustration board is the preferred choice because it is easy to cut, doesn't warp when adequately braced, and has a smooth surface that allows for a more finished look in painting. When braced, as described in Chapter Ten, it is strong enough for you to mount shelves, wall accessories, furniture, and other special effects on it without its buckling.

The edges of individual sections to be joined into an angled wall should be cut at a slant allowing the sections to come together neatly. You can cover the seam with wallpaper, fill it in with glue or Spackle, or cover it with masking or paper tape before painting. Or form the angled sections by scoring halfway through the illustration board, bending it and reinforcing the crack with tiny quarter-round molding.

Unless side walls are to be angled or include windows, doors, or recessed cupboard openings, you can work directly on the sides of the shell or apply the wall treatment to thin cardboard and glue it into place later.

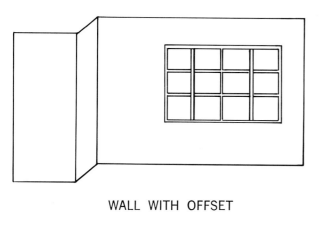

WALL WITH OFFSET

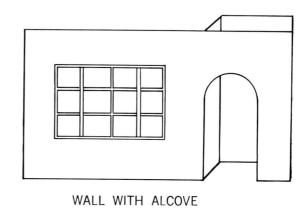

WALL WITH ALCOVE

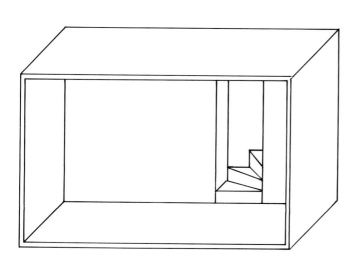

STAIRS STARTING BEHIND INTERIOR WALL

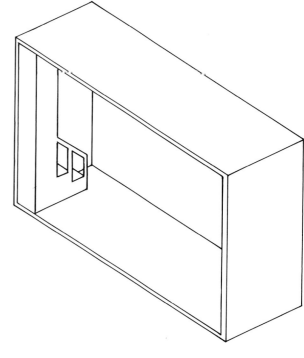

STAIRWAY ON SIDE WALL

Figure 2

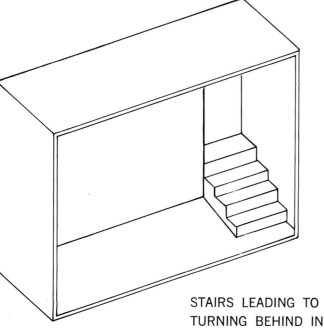

STAIRS LEADING TO BACK WALL AND
TURNING BEHIND INTERIOR WALL

Select thin woods for paneling in order to conserve space. Spray all papers used as wallpaper two or three times with clear acrylic spray, both front and back, to facilitate smooth mounting and protect the surface in gluing clean-ups. Ribbon strips and fabric with tiny motifs often provide charming wall coverings.

STAIRWAYS

Stairways are tricky in vignette dimensions, but can be included in a symbolic yet realistic manner if plotted so that the viewer cannot actually see where the stairs end. This may be accomplished by planning the stairs in such a way that they lead behind a wall section or into a blind spot (Figure 2).

WINDOWS

The size of windows varies according to the style and period being depicted. Contemporary windows can be observed and measured for their detailing and dimensions, but period subjects should be researched for authentic size and identifying features.

In reduced scale it is not necessary, nor sometimes feasible, to attempt to re-create every minute molding of the original. The basic elements of window construction should be noted—the jamb, sash, muntins, casing, special trim moldings, sill and apron, if any—but license can be taken to simplify the construction by eliminating hidden detailing or features too intricate for reduced scale.

It is sufficient in most instances to install wood framing into the wall opening, glue in the muntins that frame the window panes and add the finishing touches of casing and moldings. When choosing the wood size for construction, take into account the ⅛″ thickness of the opening in the illustration board wall.

For easier measuring, cutting, and gluing, make a pattern of the window in its reduced dimensions on graph paper. Glue it to a piece of cardboard and cover it with a see-through wax paper upon which the work can be done. This may be used for cutting the proper lengths and for squared-off and parallel assembly when gluing pieces together.

You can assemble the parts directly in the wall opening. Or construct the entire window, without its final outer molding, and insert it as a finished unit.

You can frame in the window panes in one of three ways (Figure 3).

If thin wood is used, such as ¹⁄₁₆″, full-length verticals can be over-lapped by full-length horizontals. A second approach is to cut notches in the horizontals and overlap them snugly onto full-length verticals to form the intersections. Or, cut all the horizontals to fit into the framed opening, and then cut vertical members and glue them in in-dividually between the horizontals on the same plane. The latter method is the most realistic looking but entails especially careful cutting and fitting.

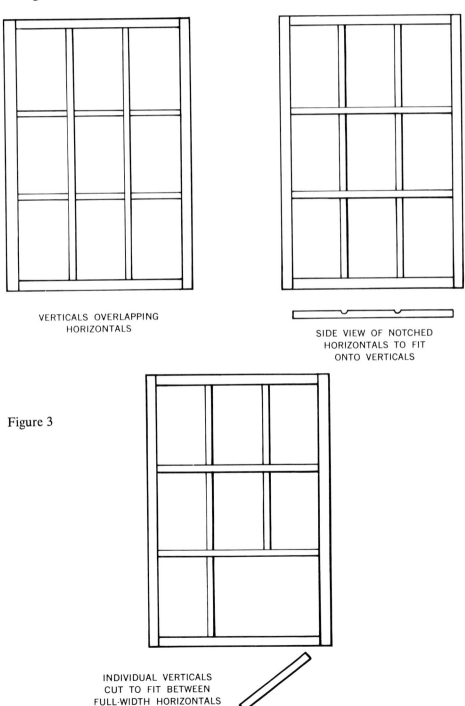

VERTICALS OVERLAPPING
HORIZONTALS

SIDE VIEW OF NOTCHED
HORIZONTALS TO FIT
ONTO VERTICALS

Figure 3

INDIVIDUAL VERTICALS
CUT TO FIT BETWEEN
FULL-WIDTH HORIZONTALS

Do any staining before installation and before gluing, as any excess glue will act as a barrier to the penetration of the stain. Painting can be done either before or after installation.

BAY WINDOWS

To construct bay windows for room and shop settings, make a center large window and two narrow side windows and install them at an angle, forming a window seat or ledge and a matching ceiling piece. A bay window might jut backward from the wall in an interior scene or extend forward if it is an exterior wall (Figure 4).

The side windows and the center window are made in three separate panels, squared off and flat, and are then installed at the angled edges of the window seat and ceiling piece (Figure 5). Use a narrower wood for window-pane framing than for the outer framing. The panels will

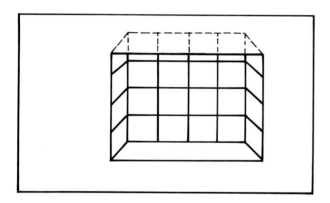
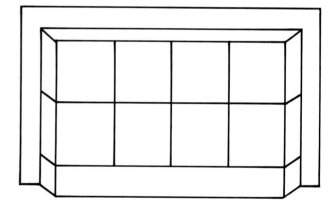

Figure 4

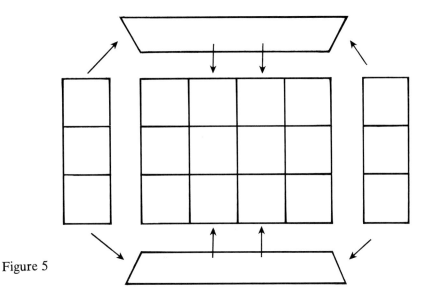

Figure 5

join at an angle and can be finished off with small quarter-round molding, either purchased or fashioned from a narrow strip of wood gently sanded into the needed shape. Install the finished bay in the wall opening, adding molding or trim to cover the seam between the window and the wall.

The window should be reinforced under the bay and over the ceiling on the hidden side of the bay wall by gluing in scrap balsa supports. The exterior bay window should be framed in with extra wall sections for support (Figure 4) or if style and period permit, decorative beams or trims can be installed above and below the bay to hold it in place.

LEADED WINDOWS

A leaded window effect can be accomplished in several ways.

You can use the soft lead that comes in a tube and apply it to a stiff clear plastic sheet in the diamond pattern. If a stained-glass effect is desired, the individual diamonds can be colored with stained-glass paints.

The leaded effect also may be simulated by etching a sheet of stiff clear plastic with the craft knife or razor blade, taking care not to cut through.

Or the window may be constructed entirely of thin strips of wood, working on the pattern with a wax paper overlay. Once assembled, coat the wood heavily with white glue, allowing it to build up slightly in the diamond points. Apply silver paint, and antiquing if desired, for a quite realistic result.

Another method is to use mesh screen of a large gauge, found in hardware stores, which can be diagonally positioned for the diamond effect. If too brilliant in its natural state, dull down the metal with metallic paint or metallic wax. Because this large-gauge screening is not very pliable, it is usually best to cut it large enough to overlap onto the hidden side of the wall opening, firmly gluing and bracing it into place with glued-in scraps of wood.

Occasionally you can find a plastic berry basket with a pattern like that of a leaded window and can cut panels of it to the required size. Apply a dull silver metallic paint and antique, if desired.

In all cases, add finishing trim after installing the window in the wall opening.

DOORS

Doors, like windows, will vary in height, width, and styling. Their detailing can be observed from actual door construction or photographs. You may simplify elaborate moldings so long as the special characteristics that identify style and period are suggested.

Panels can be scored in and routed out by knife, or individual panels with beveled edges glued on and sanded to integrate. It is not necessary to actually hinge doors, as they will be glued into a stationary position, but the suggestion of hinges can be achieved with paper and cardboard cutouts or jewelry parts, painted black or gilt depending on style and period.

If a door is to stand ajar, shorten its width slightly in the interest of conserving space, but not to such an extent that a viewer can detect the alteration.

FLOORS

Floor effects, such as wood planking, brick, tile, and marble can be worked directly on the shell, or if more convenient, on a piece of cardboard backing to be installed later.

Planking may be laid in either direction. If it is installed from side to side, the forward edge is more finished looking, but short planks that are laid front to back aid in depth perspective (Photo 13). The raw edges should be finished off neatly.

Tile is simulated by gluing down a paper with tile pattern, available from some miniature suppliers, and varnishing several times. Or you can make individual tiles, inked or painted in the desired colors on thin cardboard, cut them apart, install one by one and then varnish them. A paper with a marbleized pattern in small enough scale makes an effective counterfeit of a marble floor when tightly glued down and varnished.

In all instances before varnishing, test the papers, ink, or paint to see if color will run. This is prevented in most instances by spraying with clear acrylic spray or sealing with a half-and-half mixture of white shellac and denatured alcohol before applying varnish.

A square of real floor tile that imitates in small scale a freeform flagstone or cobblestone pattern could also be used if altered with paint to disguise the commercial tile appearance. Techniques for simulating brick and cobblestone are described later in this chapter.

CEILINGS

Ceilings may be painted directly on the interior of the shell unless they are to be slanted, in which case you should construct them of thick wood (Photo 21) or illustration board.

If the subject matter permits, the use of ceiling beams running from front to back is an effective depth-impression device (Photo 28).

DESIGNS IN RELIEF

For elaborate wainscotting, carved panels, plaster relief, friezes, and even the raised motifs on some painted furniture, use the heavy gold paper braids and designs found in découpage and craft centers. They can be cut apart and reassembled to get the desired effect. Spray them two or three times with clear acrylic spray to insure best acceptance of paint or gesso.

Paint the individual cutouts before gluing to the background surface so depressions are not excessively filled in and the raised look flattened. A final coat of paint applied after gluing will integrate the background and the raised design.

Wood and composition borders and designs, found in a few craft supply catalogs, can be incorporated, especially on building exteriors, when a heavily carved look is desired. They may be gessoed and painted. Or, you can use metal bandings and jewelry findings, the parts used in jewelry making, either as they are or gessoed and painted.

Photo 21: Early Shipping Merchant's Office, Susan Rogers Braun. 9″ x 12″ x 2¼″.
Photo: George Peterson

MOLDINGS

The addition of moldings, such as baseboards, chair rails, and ceiling trims, serves not only to hide cut edges but also to achieve a finished, professional look that enhances the realism of the vignette.

A few miniature supply sources carry such moldings ready-made in small scale, but you can create them yourself by combining various sizes of narrow strips of wood glued together and sanded to achieve shaping and integration of layers. An alternate method is to strip out levels of wood from a thick piece, and use a knife to score ornate detailings.

You can make wide moldings, such as baseboards, with thin wood or layers of thin cardboard combined with wood strips. They can be sanded and painted to integrate. Cardboard moldings cannot be stained.

Gold paper braid and bandings may be used by themselves, or in combination with wood and cardboard to obtain a raised design after they are glued together and painted.

BRICK

Two methods are suggested for simulating brick, both with most realistic results.

Incised method: draw the brick and mortar pattern on illustration board, using a razor blade or craft knife to score all the mortar lines, not cutting through the board. Then peel out the "mortar" in strips, leaving a channel between bricks. The bricks should be roughened up on the edges with a file, emery board, or sandpaper to create the irregularities present in real brick. A few gouges on the surface of the brick will represent cracks and porous openings characteristic of brick.

Brush off-white or light gray acrylic paint thickly into the mortar channels and then apply the color of the brick by brushing or wiping it on with a rag across the raised area. The brick may be toned by lightly applying and quickly wiping off black or brown paint.

Glued-on method: glue on brick size pieces of thin cardboard to a backing cardboard, allowing space for mortar channels. Roughen the brick and paint using the procedure described above.

COBBLESTONE, STONE FIREPLACES

Use small stones, like the smooth, washed ones found on beaches and chosen for their color and flatness. Press them into wet modeling or Spackle paste that has been spread on an illustration-board form representing the front of a fireplace (Photo 22) or a cobblestone street. The paste should not be used too thickly and, after the stones are imbedded and the paste dry, should be protected from flaking and cracking by brushing with white glue.

Photo 22: Cottage with Fireplace, Susan Rogers Braun. 8″ x 10″ x 3″. Photo: George Peterson

Photo 23: Braunhall, Susan Rogers Braun. 9″ x 12″ x 4½″. Photo: George Peterson

FIREPLACES

To conserve space in the depth of the vignette, the facade of a fireplace may be recessed into the wall (Photo 23). However, if you plan to have it extend out into the floor area, construct a shallow box of illustration board and glue it to the wall opening after the brick, stone, marble, or wood effect has been applied.

You can make elegant fireplaces with carved motifs by using the same techniques described earlier in this chapter for relief designs.

Inset tile can be made of cutout designs mounted on individual card-board tiles or miniature tile paper glued into position and varnished.

Behind the wall opening that accommodates the grate and logs, install a three-sided box of illustration board, slightly larger than the wall opening in width and at least two inches taller than the height of the opening. Glue it to the back of the wall and further secure it by gluing in scraps of wood that fasten to the box and wall. The effects of brick and soot are more easily applied if done first.

Outside detailing of mantels, panels, and other architectural features should be added to the front of the fireplace.

STUCCO

Rough exterior stucco can be imitated by using a thin wash of paint over gritty sandpaper which has been glued to the wall, or by sprinkling sand or salt onto an acrylic painted surface while it is still very wet. When dry, shake off the excess and spray the wall two or three times with clear acrylic spray.

Interior stuccoed walls can be simulated by using a heavy thickness of acrylic paint or gesso, lightly sprinkling it when wet with sand or salt, and when dried spraying it with clear acrylic spray. Or, you can paint the wall and while the paint is wet, press a piece of wax paper onto it and pull it away, thereby creating a textured effect.

SHINGLES

Cut individual shingles from thin cardboard, brush them with acrylic paint and while very wet, sprinkle on salt and pepper. They should then be sprayed two or three times with clear acrylic spray. Install them starting with the bottom row and overlap each succeeding row.

Cedar shake can be made of thin cardboard or wood squares with the bottom edge slashed in several places to appear splintered and irregular. The squares may be stained the desired shade and glued into position as with shingles (Photo 1).

WROUGHT IRON

Simple wrought iron designs can be imitated by bending a hairpin or wire of appropriate gauge into the desired shape and then painting it.

More elaborate wrought iron can be made by cutting out and combining motifs of heavy gold paper braids and designs, sprayed first with acrylic spray and then painted either with glossy or flat model paints, depending on the look desired.

Lightweight metal parts, found in stores selling jewelry-making supplies or in miniature supply catalogs, can be bent or cut apart with tin snips or heavy scissors and then painted.

COLUMNS

Columns protruding from an exterior building wall or in an elegant interior setting can be constructed from a cardboard tube used for wax paper, aluminum foil, and gift wraps. Cut it in half lengthwise and glue one section against the wall between a ceiling molding and a floor pedestal.

You can glue on an appropriately patterned paper for a marble or granite appearance, or counterfeit the look by stippling on wet paint with a brush and adding flecks of color and veining. If paper is used, coat it with white glue after pasting it on, and spray it a few times with clear acrylic spray or varnish it.

A fluted column can be made by gluing $\frac{1}{16}''$ by $\frac{1}{16}''$ wood strips vertically on a half tube of cardboard, sanding their edges to integrate the wood and cardboard into fluted channels and then painting heavily with acrylic paint or gesso.

9

Adapting and Making Accessories

Accessories have a significant role in the miniature vignette, for they are not only an element in developing the "story" but are a contributing factor in the total composition.

The vignette might be described as a picture using three-dimensional devices, accessories being one of the components in the arrangement of mass, line, and color.

They are the added comments that testify to modes and manners of past and present life styles and can function to illustrate the habits and interests of either the unseen "occupant" or the vignettist.

They play a role in the plotting of color accents, and discriminatingly selected, help to impart information about mood, time, place, and ownership. Is the setting an austere room of dramatically stark furnishings or a cozy, warm one filled with color and light? Is it formal and elegant, or rustic? The domain of a man, woman, or child? Modern or period? The shop of a milliner or a pharmacist?

A few accessories, thoughtfully arranged, are more effective than many placed in a haphazard or random manner. The goal should be to create a picture of real life in miniature scale rather than merely to display a collection of interesting diminutive objects.

ADAPTING NOVELTIES

Each accessory should be put to the tests of scale, color, and surface qualities if realism is to be the result. Good miniatures have become

more available in recent years and many can be used without alterations, but even the most inexpensive models can be considered. Many
of the tiny replicas of full size objects found in gum ball machines, doll
house departments, novelty and party goods stores have fine detailing,
though they are usually made of unrealistic materials.

The clever vignettist will see beyond the falseness of color and artificial materials to the possibilities of adapting such miniatures, here
shown before and after (Photos 24, 25 and 26). A perceptive eye, a
little ingenuity and often just a few dabs of paint can transform even a
cheap counterfeit into a realistic miniature.

An in-scale plastic shovel, for instance, becomes a true-to-life miniature with the application of flat black model or acrylic paint. Behind the
vignette glass the observer will not detect that it is not truly metal. If
the shovel is already black, you should paint it to change the fake
plastic surface into a lifelike, dull metal one.

Photos 24, 25, 26: Adaptation of Novelty Items. Photo: Fred Slater

Jewelry miniatures and party trinkets may have unwanted features, such as charm rings, that can be snipped or sawed off. A too large miniature sometimes can be cut down and reduced to the proper scale, or it may be dismantled into parts that can be used separately or assembled with other pieces into an unusual accessory.

Amid the flotsam of cast-off articles, there sometimes hides a needed accessory, but "cute" conversions of too thick buttons into plates, or toothpaste caps into boudoir lamp shades should be shunned. Only if you can truly disguise such items should they be considered.

When remedial painting and alterations fail to turn a novelty into an authentic reproduction, it should be eliminated from the plan and another one searched for to take its place. And always keep in mind the possibility of making it from scratch.

MAKING MINIATURES

A vignette that has been merely put together from an assemblage of purchased, unretouched miniatures fails in the goal of realism and will lack the stamp of the vignettist's creativity. Even if you can find all the required miniatures commercially, items should be included that are custom crafted, not only for the sheer fun and challenge involved but to achieve a uniquely personalized and artistic three-dimensional picture.

When purchased items and well-made originals are used side by side, they tend to complement each other. Ready-mades in good scale and with substantially lifelike textures add credibility to a setting. The home-crafted miniatures make an overall contribution to individuality and broaden the scope of possibilities in the story or theme.

The techniques described in this chapter for making accessories are *concepts* pointing out the use of a variety of materials from sometimes unlikely sources. They can be applied in many ways and should stimulate you to explore the possibilities for inventing a needed accessory not mentioned here.

BASIC INSTRUCTIONS

A few general instructions will help in handling various materials.

Plastic and metal: You can use water-base acrylic paints or model enamels, although when using acrylic, avoid excessive handling after painting because the painted surface is easily marred and scratched.

Plastic and metal surfaces will receive acrylic paints better if first sprayed with clear acrylic spray. Use white glue to join plastic to plastic, or plastic to other surfaces, porous or solid. Use a clear craft cement, jewelry or household types, to join lightweight metals. Either white glue or one of the cements can be used to glue metal to other surfaces, depending upon the weight of the metal piece and amount of gluing surface. Occasionally it is necessary to use epoxy glue for a good bond of heavyweight metals. Cements can disturb painted surfaces, so they should be applied neatly and sparingly to avoid damage.

Wood: You can use any paint. White glue provides good adhesion of two wood surfaces and wood to other surfaces, except in some instances of joining wood and metal. Then use a clear craft cement.

Paper: White glue, applied thinly and evenly, or the mucilage sold in découpage shops for paper work are the best choices. Rubber cement tends to bleed through with a stain as it ages. If paper is very thin, spray the back two or three times with acrylic spray to keep glue from soaking through.

Fabric: Use white glue or glues made specifically for fabric work. When gluing fabric to another surface, spray the back three or four times with clear acrylic spray to prevent glue from oozing through and staining the top surface. Fabric contents vary so much that it is best to conduct a preliminary test with a small scrap. Cotton fabrics, but not the synthetics, can be aged and colors muted by immersion in household bleach for a few minutes, or by soaking in strong tea or coffee.

MODELED ACCESSORIES

Many items that cannot be obtained in any other way can be made with modeling compounds. The best type is one that is maleable and soft while shaping and then is baked to permanent hardness in about 15 minutes in a moderate oven. It can be sanded, sawed, cut with a knife, carved, and painted, but not with lacquer.

It is fairly easy to sculpt, though some items may require a little practice. Though hundreds of objects can be modeled as skill increases, some examples (Figure 6) to illustrate a range of ideas are vegetables, fruits, baked goods and other food stuffs, dishes, opaque bottles, jugs, dress forms, small statuary and busts, lavabos, teddy bear forms (to be furred later with yarn fuzz), dolls, "ceramic" cannisters.

Craftsmen proficient in clay may choose to model in this medium. Homemade bread dough mixes are not recommended because of the

MODELED ACCESSORIES

Figure 6

CAULIFLOWER

ORANGES

CARROTS

BREAD

PIE

ROLLS

TIERED CAKE

WINE BOTTLE

JUG

TEDDY BEAR FORM

PIPE

BUST

TOBY MUG

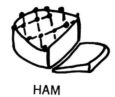

HAM

CROCKERY

possibility that bugs or mold may develop later; however, if you do choose to use them, varnish them as an added protection. Do not include real food products, such as corn flakes used as leaves.

BOOKS

Book covers and jackets (Figure 7): Cut out a book cover slightly larger than the miniature page size from heavy paper or an old greeting card, and then cover it with a book jacket designed from appropriate gift wrap papers, magazine cutouts, or decorative papers thin enough not to crack when folded. Wrap the book jacket around the cover, as illustrated, in the same fashion as putting a jacket on a full-size book. Allow it to be loose around the spine but paste its edges on the inside of the covers. Titles can be provided by handlettering or pasting on tiny cutouts. Thin supple leathers can be used to make finished jackets but because of their thickness need not be applied to separate covers.

Closed books when contents will not show (Figure 8): Cut up pieces of balsa wood or glue together several thicknesses of cardboard into page size and content depth. Paint the edges white or brush them lightly with gilt. Then glue the contents into a slightly larger finished book cover.

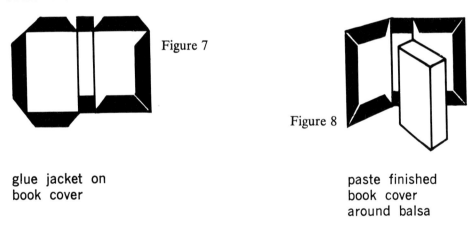

Figure 7

Figure 8

glue jacket on
book cover

paste finished
book cover
around balsa

Books in which page edges will be noticeable (Figure 9): Rule out miniature pages on typing paper or other thin stock, cut them apart and stack. Holding the pages in a neat bundle, dip one edge into white glue and place into the finished book cover. If desired, the page edges can be lightly brushed with gilt.

Books to be left open with inner pages on view (Figure 10): Glue two thin stacks of individual paper pages onto each inner side of a

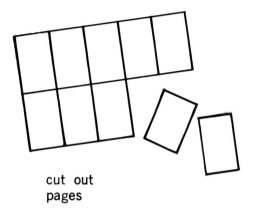

cut out
pages

Figure 9

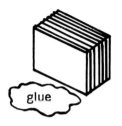

hold in bundle
and dip one
edge in glue

place glued edge
of bundle on
inner spine of
book jacket

Figure 10

glue in special
pages of tiny
pictures and
print

finished book cover, and tip in an inner double page glued only at the center fold. Tiny in-scale pictures and print, often found in small advertisements, can comprise the center fold or be glued individually onto the pages. Turn a few page edges slightly for a loose, unglued appearance.

EYEGLASSES (FIGURE 11)

The frames may be made of thin gauge wire, such as that found in plastic bag ties with paper peeled off. Form them with a looping motion, starting with one ear piece and working in order to the other side. Minor adjustments can be made with a small pliers if necessary. If you wish to add "glass," small rounds of clear cellophane or plastic can be glued to the back of the lens framing.

EYEGLASSES

Figure 11

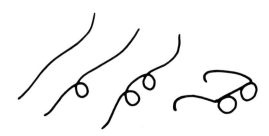

BRASS MUG (FIGURE 12)

A simple brass mug can be made of a small spent bullet shell and half of a jump ring, a part used in jewelry making. Cut the ring with a wire cutter and glue one half onto the shell with clear cement to form the handle.

BRASS MUG

Figure 12

ANTIQUE CANDLEHOLDERS (FIGURE 13)

Attractive antique candleholders, in tall and short styles, can be assembled from an assortment of small jewelry findings, such as bead separators, jump rings, small rivets or eyelets, tiny washers, ornate tacks with nail removed by wire cutter. Use clear craft glue.

ANTIQUE CANDLEHOLDERS

Figure 13

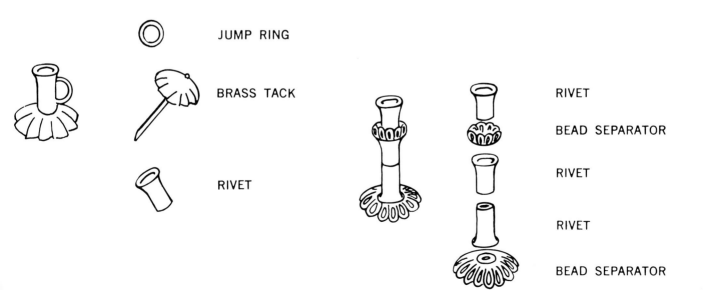

ELEGANT PERFUME BOTTLES (FIGURE 14)

Select pearl, crystal, jade, filigree, brass and other kinds of beads for their faceting, overall shape, and authentic appearance. Combine them with small washers, bead separators, and tiny rivets.

An opaque bottle, such as one that looks like porcelain, can be shaped out of balsa wood or basswood, painted with glossy enamel, or acrylic paint followed by a coating of white glue. Decorative paper cutouts can be pasted onto the bottle, then coated with white glue or brushed with satin varnish or clear nail polish. Protect the cutouts from color change with sealer or two or three coats of clear acrylic spray.

ELEGANT PERFUME BOTTLES

 BRASS BEAD

 RIVET

BEAD SEPARATOR

 FILIGREE METAL BEAD

Figure 14

 FACETED CRYSTAL TEARDROP BEAD

 BEAD SEPARATOR

 FACETED CRYSTAL BEAD

UNUSUAL PLATES (PHOTO 27)

Paint a wood or plastic dish, one of modeling compound, or a suitably shaped, thin button with holes filled in with wood fill or spackle. Then decorate it with tiny cutouts from stamps, gift wrap, catalogs, magazines, imported candy wrappers. A coating of white glue may give the desired effect, or the dish can be varnished or brushed with clear nail polish if the cutouts have been sealed as described above.

Photo 27: Decorated Plates from Novelty Dishes. Photo: Fred Slater

FRUIT CRATE (FIGURE 15)

Use either thin, unsanded wood or wood of a matchbox with paper peeled off. If a damp cloth is used to remove the paper covering, the wood will fuzz up, approximating the characteristic of wood in a real fruit crate. If the wood warps, blot and press until dry before cutting and constructing the crate.

FRUIT CRATE

Figure 15

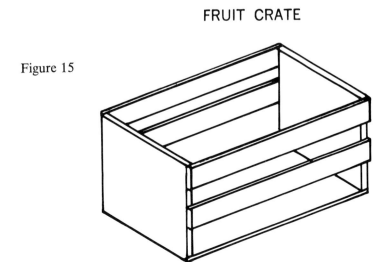

CUPBOARDS AND CURIO CABINETS (FIGURE 16)

Interesting small cupboards and ornate hanging curio wall cabinets can be made of layers of thin cardboard laminated to the proper thickness and sturdiness. For a raised relief, glue on scrolled motifs and bandings cut out from gold paper braids, sprayed first with clear acrylic, then painted the color of the cabinet. A final coating of paint after pasting will integrate the carved effects to the case. Nylon net fabric painted black or silver can be used in door openings to simulate screening.

HANGING CUPBOARD

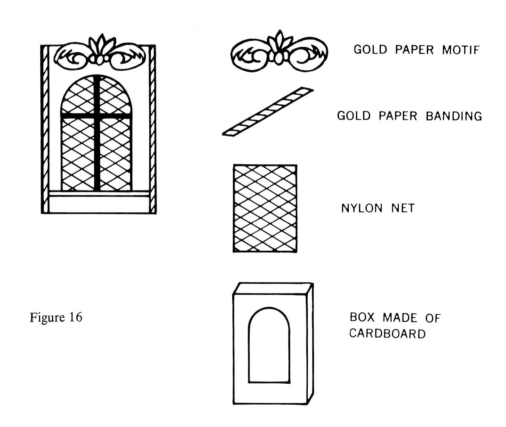

GOLD PAPER MOTIF

GOLD PAPER BANDING

NYLON NET

Figure 16

BOX MADE OF CARDBOARD

CANNED GOODS

Cut wood doweling of the correct diameter to represent large or small cans to the proper length, paint the ends silver, and glue on labels in small reduction found in magazine food advertisements and from miniature suppliers.

RUGS

A variety of possibilities present themselves for making rugs. Sometimes you can find a fabric in which the nap, texture, and pattern are in appropriate scale. Needlepointers can make an original rug design using petit point canvas. Velveteen, stretched taut while gluing down, imitates rich-looking, elegant carpeting. Early American style braided rugs can be crocheted on a tiny hook with embroidery floss, or you can use lightweight yarns, or fine string that has been shaded with colored pencils, coiling it around and around as you glue it on wax paper or paper backing. Then press it as flat as possible. In some vignettes, it is not out of place to use paper rugs found in magazine illustrations. Darken their cut edges with colored pencils.

CURTAINS

Curtains and draperies are often eliminated in vignettes unless specifically needed for effect. They fill up the available space and obstruct too much of the view of a background scene. When used, install them in a flat, pleated manner using soft, pliable fabrics, ribbons, or laces that will not be too bulky. The bare window with its finished moldings, and perhaps a valance, is usually preferred.

HARDWARE (FIGURE 17)

Drawer pulls, handles, and lock plates on furniture, if they cannot be found ready-made from miniature suppliers, may be improvised from jewelry findings, hooks and eyes used by seamstresses, nails, pins, and tiny motifs cut from gold paper braid that have been antiqued or painted. Gold braids and gold doily cutouts may be silvered by rubbing the surface with acetone or nail polish remover. For a pewter look, dull the silver by lightly wiping on black paint or wood stain.

HARDWARE

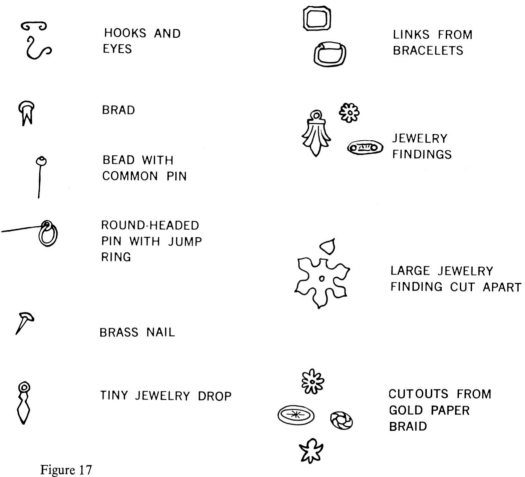

Figure 17

10

Assembling the Vignette

The steps outlined in this chapter give the order of assembly that generally is followed for most vignettes. If the back wall of the vignette is worked or installed directly on the shell, assembly starts with Step Three.

There may be varying elements in an individual design plan which necessitate a change in the usual order. For example, a vignette in which the viewer is looking through the exterior of a shop requires the main interior wall to be positioned in front *after* the side walls, furnishings, and accessories are put into place (Photo 10).

The eleven steps in the order of assembly are:
1. Background print
2. Buttressing
3. Rear wall
4. Side walls
5. Ceiling
6. Floors
7. Moldings
8. Furniture
9. Accessories
10. Finishing touches
11. Lockup

A vignette whose basic elements have been carefully measured and cut can be assembled without gluing to give the interior plan a "dry run" before permanent installation. Everything can be held temporarily in place with mounting adhesive. This enables you to find out if the usual order of assembly should be rearranged for a particular project, and allows for alterations and corrections before gluing.

It is a good idea to "live with" the vignette a day or so before permanent gluing. Hold the frame in front of the shell, study the vignette several times, move it from one lighting situation to another, give it a critical examination for compositional elements, and add or subtract objects if desired.

STEP 1—BACKGROUND PRINT

Sections in Chapter Four tell how to place the print in the shell for proper perspective and how to enlarge the background if necessary to keep edges hidden. If your plan calls for a door or window in a corner, be sure to extend the print around from the back to the side wall. These openings must be considered in painted and "constructed" backgrounds, too.

Before gluing in the print, spray it two or three times front and back with clear acrylic spray to aid in smoother gluing, especially of thin papers. Cover the back of the print completely with white glue or découpage mucilage, leaving no dry spots. Set the print into the shell in its proper position and push out any air pockets, working from the center to the outer edges. The print is likely to buckle later if glued only along the edges.

Any outdoor effects, such as trees, shrubbery, flowers, fences, and other devices to interrupt the viewer's line of sight through a window or door should be installed at this point. Remember that you are working in a space that is limited to the distance between the back wall of the shell and the rear wall of the setting.

STEP 2—BUTTRESSING

Free-standing interior walls must be supported as much as possible to prevent shifting and buckling. Buttressing, or bracing, is provided by gluing in strips of balsa wood in every spot along the inside perimeter of the shell and other points behind the wall (Figure 18) where it will not be visible through wall openings. In case it will be seen, you should disguise the buttressing with a treatment compatible to the subject matter. You might cover it with foliage or treat it as a garden wall or exterior building protrusion with brick, stone, or siding.

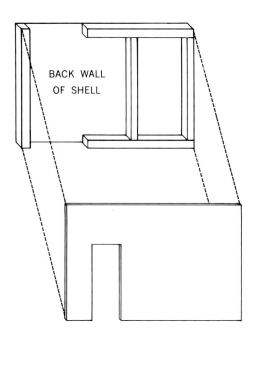

Figure 18

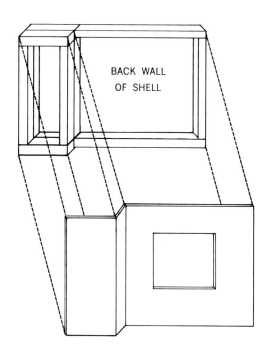

Choose wood strips or combinations of them that are the same depth as the space between the wall and the background. In general, it is sufficient to figure on a depth of ½″, but this may vary according to the design plan and how much total working space there is in a given shell. Deeper buttressing is usually required for fireplaces, stairways, and walls with alcoves or offsets. The buttressing should provide as much of a ledge as possible for gluing the wall in. The best width is ½ ", although you can use ¼ "-wide balsa in areas where wider braces would show.

Counterbracing is provided on the front side of a free-standing wall when side walls, floors and ceilings made as separate units, furniture, molding, and shelving are glued in place. It is the combination of buttressing from behind and counterbracing in front that provides a tight interlocking assembly that will prevent buckling of the wall.

STEP 3—REAR WALL

Using white glue, fasten the rear wall with completed windows and door framing securely to the buttressing. This bracing is not necessary, of course, if the wall treatment is worked directly on the shell, or if it is a wall unit to be installed as a separate piece and glued flat to the shell. Various wall treatments are described in Chapter Eight.

STEP 4—SIDE WALLS

Angled side walls constructed of illustration board must be supported with buttressing cut to the shape of the angle. If your plan for the side walls calls for paneling, heavy painting, or wallpapering directly on the shell, permanently glue in the rear wall first—it will not slide in after the side walls have been worked on. If the wall treatment has been applied to illustration board or thin cardboard, install these separate units against the shell wall, covering the backs completely with glue. Hold them in place until the glue sets up, and their edges will not pull away from the shell. The forward edges of side walls should be neatly finished off with paint or the wallpaper used in the interior unless they are to be covered by molding. Side walls are discussed in Chapter Eight.

STEP 5—CEILING

You can paint most ceilings directly on the shell unless a special effect, such as angling, is planned. A slanted ceiling can be made of illustration board or thick wood and glued onto buttressing that has been cut with an angled edge to conform to the slant of the ceiling. Ceiling beams are mentioned in Chapter Eight.

STEP 6—FLOOR

If you work on the floor of the shell directly with planking, tile, marble, brick, or cobblestone effects, the back and side walls should be installed first, unless the floor is planned to extend under the side walls. Separate floor pieces with any of these treatments, discussed in Chapter Eight, may be glued in after the walls are installed if they are cut to fit within them. Finish off the forward visible edge of the floor neatly.

STEP 7—MOLDINGS

Glue in ceilings moldings, beams, baseboards, chair rails, and the other architectural detailing that not only adds a professional touch to the vignette but helps to hide slight irregularities in cutting, papering, and painting. In many cases, these details also serve to countersupport free-standing and angled walls. Techniques for making moldings are given in Chapter Eight.

STEP 8—FURNITURE

Glue in furniture pieces wherever they touch the walls or floor. If a piece is to be placed in an angled position, try to arrange it in such a manner that an edge touches a wall and provides an additional gluing contact. Free-standing furniture can be glued by the feet only, but if the weight requires it and the design of the feet permits, insert tiny sequin pins with heads cut off into the feet and flooring, in addition to gluing. Glue a scrap of wood to the unexposed side of a design if it has an overhanging top, such as a bureau or cabinet, to fill in the space between the wall and back panel and thus provide an enlarged gluing area.

Lightweight metal furniture, for instance an ice cream parlor chair, should be glued onto a smooth, not a fabric, surface with clear craft glue. The gluing area of the chair's looped wire feet is so minute that it is advisable to anchor them to the floor with a small inverted U-shaped piece of wire glued through the loop of the feet into the flooring. Use epoxy glue for heavier metal designs. A piece of furniture with a hollow base, such as an ice cream parlor table whose pedestal was made with a large metal candlestick, should have its gluing surface increased by filling in the hollow with wood.

All furniture should be glued at as many points of contact to floors and walls as possible without the slightest trace of glue showing. Glue permanently the drawers and cupboard doors that could fall out or swing open after the vignette is sealed.

STEP 9—ACCESSORIES

The basic instructions given in Chapter Nine for joining various surfaces with the best choice of glue are guidelines to follow for permanently installing accessories in the vignette.

STEP 10—FINISHING TOUCHES

If the forward, visible edges of side walls, floor, and ceiling have not been finished to coordinate with the interior, hide them behind a thin molding, preferably ¹⁄₃₂″ thick basswood or balsa, appropriately stained or painted. The molding, however, must not extend forward from the shell opening to interfere with the lay of the glass on the shell edges. Gold paper braid may also be used for a finishing molding if it integrates with the design and subject matter.

As with any artwork of which the artist is justifiably proud, the vignette is signed in an unobstrusive yet visible spot, as in the music room (Photo 17).

A final professional-looking touch is added by fastening to the frame or outer side of the shell a small brass plate engraved with the title, your name, and perhaps the year the work was completed. It may be ordered from art shops and some hardware stores.

STEP 11—LOCKUP

The best types of hardware to use for fastening the frame to the shell are described in Chapter Six. Use screws to mount hinges, for hammering in nails can jar loose fragile furniture and accessories, and nails have a tendency to pull out under the weight of the vignette. The screws should be as long as possible, yet not intrude visibly into the vignette interior. Start screw holes with an awl or ice pick; no hammering is necessary.

Fasten the glass into the finished frame with silicone seal or clear craft glue, or put it in loose to permit photographing without reflective glare.

PART 3
FURNITURE

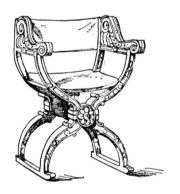

11

Adapting Ready-made Furniture

Miniature furniture may be constructed in scale with the help of the techniques described in the next chapter, or the vignettist may choose to work with ready-made designs available in the marketplace. The majority of miniature furniture production is in 1″ scale, and though not all pieces will qualify for use in the space limitations of a vignette, many pieces fit well into vignettes if adapted to meet the demands for realism, authenticity, and economy of space. To accomplish this some of them must undergo modifications in line, bulk, and finish.

Sometimes furniture saved from an old doll house meets the criteria for use in a vignette. Another source is custom furniture made by a few skilled miniaturists and sold by catalog. Some of these craftsmen accept orders for one-of-a-kind pieces. Though such furniture is usually a relatively expensive investment, the vignette approach affords an excellent and safe showcase for an outstanding collector's item.

It is usually best to avoid plastic furniture, but clever vignettists have accomplished remarkable results with paints and redesigning that disguise the undesirable plastic properties. Do not use heavy cast iron pieces, as they are too difficult to fasten in securely and their weight can throw the vignette off-balance if it is to be hung.

Doll house furniture is made sturdy enough to hold up in play and handling, a quality not necessary in vignette use. The woods are harder than the balsa, thin basswood, and laminated cardboards recommended for the vignettist's custom designs, but in spite of this, many modifications can be accomplished with the usual tools.

If the lines of a ready-made piece are too bulky, and thick, especially evident in legs, table tops, and ornamentation, you can scale them down by using the craft knife with a sharp blade as a whittling tool to chip and shave off unwanted wood, to bevel edges, and sometimes even to reshape a part. Use a saw to cut off undesirable features or to separate a large piece into two or three furniture units, a case in point being the hanging cabinet in the gardener's shed (Photo 28) which actually is the hutch separated from the table base of a tall cabinet. The table was used later by the vignettist in another project.

Photo 28: Gardener's Shed, Muriel Hoffman, The Beehive Studio. 9″ x 12″ x 5½″. Photo: George Peterson

Heavy sanding with coarse sandpaper will thin down visible edges and overly thick panels for more graceful proportions and will eliminate the machined look. Tops of tables, cabinets, and chests of drawers that overhang the back of the design where it is to be glued against a wall can be sawed off in the interest of conserving space in the depth, and to aid in firmer gluing.

A close-up of the cupboard (Photo 29) in the farm house (Photo 16) illustrates how a doll house piece (Photo 30) was altered to reduce its bulky edges and give it a patina that suggests an old piece, long used and often polished. The visible edges were thinned and slightly rounded for a worn look, both by shaving with the craft knife and by sanding. Depressions suggesting age were incorporated, and the entire piece was

Photo 29: Altered Doll House Cupboard. Photo: Fred Slater

Photo 30: Doll House Cupboard Before Adaptation. Photo: Fred Slater

heavily sanded and restained. Finally, subtle antiquing was applied to wood and hardware to suggest that this little cupboard had been handed down from one generation to the next.

You can use custom made and commercial furniture together in the same vignette provided period, style, and finish complement each other. The Windsor chair and sheet music stand in the music room (Photo 17) are doll house pieces scaled down and restained to go with the corner cupboard made of balsa wood.

You can prepare unvarnished but stained furniture for a new shade of staining by sanding, first with coarse sandpaper and then extra fine sandpaper to restore a smooth surface.

A varnished design usually requires only a heavy sanding and sometimes a little scraping to remove the gloss to prepare it for restaining. If a piece is heavily varnished, you might want to try a commercial remover, the type used for full-size furniture, to strip it; however, this is rarely necessary. If it is to be painted, the varnish need not be removed completely, though the surface should be roughened up by sanding.

You can remove wax from furniture by wiping it off with turpentine.

It is often desirable to change drawer pulls on commercial pieces to achieve authenticity of a given style or period. If new hardware cannot be found from miniature supply catalogs or stores carrying miniatures, you will find the techniques for making drawer pulls discussed and illustrated in Chapter Nine helpful.

The addition of small detailing sometimes lacking on purchased miniatures can transform doll house playthings into more realistic objects—for example, cutting in the lines of staves in barrels (Photo 31) and wooden buckets, antiquing, adding "metal" bandings of silver paper.

Photo 31: Realistic Details Added to Novelty Barrel.
Photo: Fred Slater

Simple wood pieces can be handsomely altered in appearance and decorative function by adding narrow wood moldings, or gold paper bandings and raised relief motifs which, after painting, simulate carving. Often you can give a plain wood piece a new role and place it in an elegant setting simply by painting and antiquing.

The beauty of the decorative arts in furniture is especially exemplified in embellishments of scroll, bird, fruit, and flower motifs which you can achieve either by handpainting or by pasting on tiny paper cutouts (Photos 32 and 33). Seal the designs with equal parts of white shellac and denatured alcohol and then coat with two or three layers of varnish.

Photo 32: Découpaged Secretary, Laura Davis, The Beehive Studio. Photo: George Peterson

Photo 33: Découpaged Chest, Susan Rogers Braun. Photo: George Peterson

12

Making Your Own
Furniture

If vignettes have opened up a whole new world of creative pleasure, so too does the making of miniature furniture offer new dimensions of challenge and fulfillment.

The advantages are manifold in custom crafting miniature furniture. The vignettist has complete control of scale, finish, and authenticity of line. Quality is set by your own standards of craftsmanship. The subject matter is not limited to only those pieces available on the market and you are not impeded in a current project by a time-consuming and possibly futile search for a specified miniature. The savings are substantial, for only a few pennies worth of scraps are required to turn out a handsome miniature design whose store-bought counterpart is tagged at several dollars.

This chapter, while offering the craftsman several specific designs, is intended to present techniques using various materials that make it possible for you to copy many designs of your own choosing.

Each approach should be carefully studied to learn how these materials are manipulated and used in unique applications.

The tools used are those employed in the construction of the vignette —the craft knife, razor saw, and razor blade. A set of needle files found at hobby and craft stores is helpful for working on designs with scrolls, carving, and intricate detailing. They may be used in many instances in place of or in conjunction with sandpapering, as in shaping turnings on table pedestals and chair legs. Some operations are handily accomplished with an emery board.

The materials suggested are balsa and basswood, illustration board and thin cardboards, employing methods that promise far more than elementary-looking pasteboard or crude wood pieces. The artful control of these common supplies results in fine little designs worthy of a place in a project of the most discriminating vignettist.

The furniture you make following these techniques with the suggested materials is explicitly for protected use, such as vignettes, shadow boxes, or behind the glass of curio cabinets. Most of the pieces are too fragile for extensive handling.

The beginner should not attempt furniture with elaborate carving and fretwork, or features that in reduction are extremely thin and fragile. With practice and increasing skill such details can be attempted later.

Many intricate features and ornamentation can be eliminated or modified so long as the innate feeling and essential identifying properties of the original are not destroyed.

The main characteristics to be kept intact in a miniature copy are the silhouette, giving size and basic shape, and the distinctive features that establish period and use.

GUIDELINES

The thickness of materials and the manner of assembly should be carefully considered. The inexperienced furniture maker often does not take into proper account the thickness of panels, with the consequence that individual parts when assembled come together into a piece whose overall dimensions have "grown." The expansion may be only $\frac{1}{16}''$ here and there; but the result is an out-of-scale piece.

Work only with finely sharpened pencils, for even the thickness of markings made by a dull pencil, when multiplied several times, can throw measurements off to a degree that enlarges the work and results in poor cutting and fitting.

As with the plan of a vignette interior, faithful scale reduction in furniture making is important, but in consideration of gaining even minute fractions of an inch in the restricted depth of a vignette, license *is* taken with depth dimensions whenever possible without obvious distortion.

You can shorten the depth measurements in your design of pieces that are to be seen from the front only, and completely delete the overhanging back edge of top surfaces, such as those of cabinets and chests.

Eliminate decorative moldings on the back or side of a piece where it is to be glued against a wall, and make the depths of table tops and seating units imperceptibly shallower than the full-size designs. Curved legs on the backs of chairs which will be seen only from the front may be slightly less flared than the originals.

Exposed edges of tables and shelves should be made in good proportion with fidelity to scale. If it is not practical to use wood of appropriate thinness, use thicker woods and thin or bevel exposed edges.

To bevel, first shave the edges at a 45-degree angle, and then, while holding the piece of wood flat on the work surface, briskly sand back and forth with a folded scrap of sandpaper held flat against the angled edge (Photo 34). Round table tops may be beveled in the same way.

Inlaid borders may be simulated by gluing a narrow wood banding against a routed-out edge of the top surface (Photo 35). Or, you can glue paper borders and motifs to the surface and bury them under two or three coats of varnish. If they are too thick to achieve an inlaid effect, peel or sand off the backing layers of paper.

You can make realistic marble tops for tables and bureaus by covering a piece of wood or sturdy cardboard with marbleized paper and coating it with white glue or varnish, or by counterfeiting the marble look with paints.

Photo 34: Sanding Completes Beveled Edge. Photo: Fred Slater

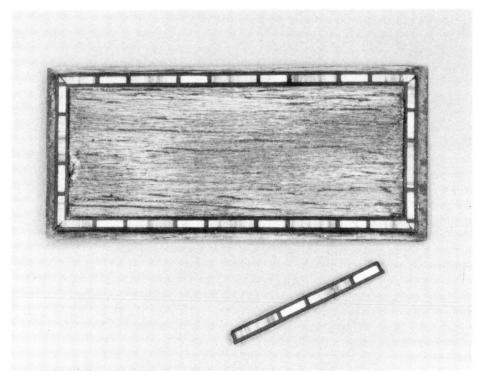

Photo 35: Decorative Molding Inlaid in Table Top. Photo: Fred Slater

The designs for table and chair legs, pedestals and balusters, when two or more matching pieces are required, should be sketched out on graph paper, indicating tapered sections and turnings (Figure 19). Use this pattern for each piece so they will match exactly. The length of wood you use can be slightly longer than necessary to get a "handle" on the work; the excess is cut off before assembling.

With the knife, score each post by rotating it under your fingers on top of the pattern. Chip out the waste wood around turnings. This gives you a roughly hewn post that can then be finished by sanding or filing to the desired size, shape, and smoothness. It is a much easier method and gives finer results, especially with balsa wood, than attempting to carve out all the features.

Ornamental cabriole legs and delicately slender ones, such as those of Queen Anne designs, are more difficult and require greater patience and practice than a straight-line style like square tapered Hepplewhite legs, or William and Mary legs, whose turnings are stacked vertically.

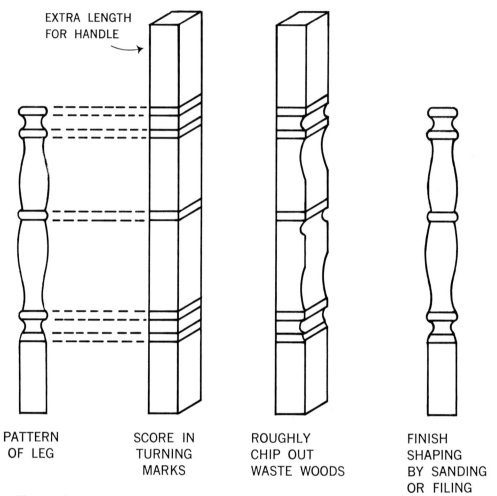

EXTRA LENGTH
FOR HANDLE →

PATTERN   SCORE IN   ROUGHLY   FINISH
OF LEG   TURNING   CHIP OUT   SHAPING
                 MARKS   WASTE WOODS   BY SANDING
                                                    OR FILING

Figure 19

Cabinets and chests of drawers are usually patterned so the cut edges appear on the side rather than the front of the piece when the parts are assembled. You can make exceptions, however, and an example is shown in the slant top desk (Photo 36) in which the end cuts of the side pieces appear in the front. You can use decorative banding or deep staining to imitate inlaid or "painted" borders on these edges.

It is possible to achieve almost invisible seams in joining front and side panels if you laminate thin woods, such as $\frac{1}{32}''$ or $\frac{1}{16}''$, to wood or thick cardboard forms and lightly sand the glued-together edges.

Curved and sculptured edges, like those of some table aprons or the decorative top piece of an Early American hutch where the scrolled

Photo 36: American Slant Top Desk. Photo: Fred Slater

design must be repeated exactly on both sides, are handily accomplished with the folded paper technique. Fold a piece of paper the size of the furniture part in half, and draw the design. Cut it out while the paper is folded. When opened, you will have the full pattern with matching repeats.

Intricate curves should be laid out along the grain of the wood. Pick through the design lightly with the pointed tip of the blade, and then remove small sections one at a time. You court the possibility of splintering or breaking the finer details if you attempt to cut out the whole curved design in one operation.

The folded paper technique is also an aid in patterning ovals, such as those that might be required as door panels or table tops. You can draw circles with a compass or trace an object of the correct diameter.

The material used to produce the arched bow of a chair, like the Windsor chair in the cottage (Photo 22), is a length of wicker, available at some hobby stores or pulled out of an old basket. You shape it by soaking it in water for 10 minutes, tying it with string into the desired curve, and drying it under a heavy weight or with its two "legs" anchored in a thick piece of balsa or Styrofoam. It can be stained to match the balsa used for the other parts of the chair.

PATTERNS

Not all furniture designs to be copied in miniature require a pattern, especially simple and straight-line pieces. A sketch and a listing of the dimensions may do. But for the beginning furniture maker and for complex designs, a pattern has the advantage of aiding you to visualize all the needed parts and to figure measurements of each component. Patterning helps you to simplify the lines and eliminate or modify details that scale reduction requires.

It is a fortunate discovery if you can find a drawing or photograph of the piece you want to copy that already is the correct size and shown in a straight-on frontal view. They may be found occasionally in furniture books, magazines, catalogs, and advertisements.

If copying an actual full-size piece of furniture, you can get the needed dimensions with ruler and yardstick measuring. Measurements can also be found in some furniture books or in issues of *Antiques* magazine, *The Connoisseur*, and the Craft House catalog of Williamsburg Reproductions.

A few books present measured drawings of designs in full scale and you need only recalculate the dimensions to the chosen scale. Two books by Lester Margon, *Masterpieces of American Furniture* (1965) and *More American Furniture Treasures* (1971), both published by the Architectural Book Publishing Company, include a considerable number of measured drawings and superb photographs. Another reference source is John G. Shea's *The American Shakers and their Furniture* (1971), published by Van Nostrand Reinhold Company, which contains measured drawings and photographs of museum classics. *The Cabinetmaker's Treasury* by F. E. Hoard and A. W. Marlow, published by The Macmillan Company, 1952, includes working drawings of many fine furniture pieces. These books are also invaluable resources for the authentic data the perfectionist vignettist seeks in the research for a period project.

Graph paper is an expediency in drafting the miniature pattern. Once you have drawn the necessary views, the pattern may be cut out; or if it is to be kept on file for reference, you can make tracings of the individual pattern parts. If you desire sturdier templates than paper or cardboard, cut them out of thin, stiff transparent plastic from the lids of greeting card boxes.

If you are trying to develop a pattern in which the dimensions of the original are not known, you can be guided by observation of size relationships evident in a photograph or drawing.

For example, in the rough sketch (Figure 20) of a lowboy with William and Mary legs, you can see that the width and the height of the piece are about the same. The length of the legs can be estimated by noting that they are slightly longer than half of the total height. You

WILLIAM AND MARY LOWBOY
rough sketch from magazine photograph

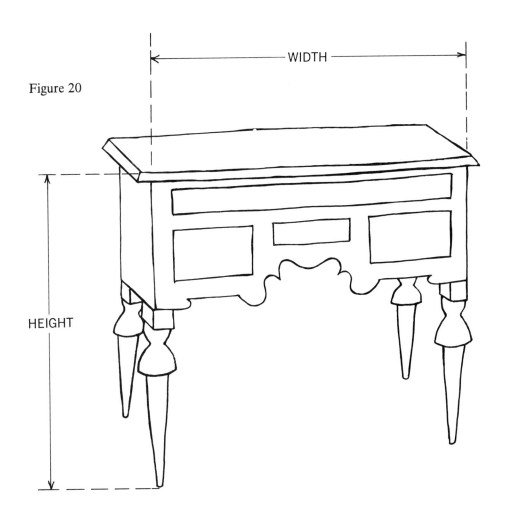

Figure 20

can see that the table top slightly overhangs the case and has a beveled edge. The relative size and shape of drawers is apparent and will not be difficult to position.

The height in miniature was assigned at 3″. If the lowboy is to be used full face in the vignette, its depth measurement can be slightly less than true depth.

The pattern (Figure 21) of the lowboy (Photo 37) consists of a front view, one side view, and a top view. All three views are often necessary to indicate the proper dimensions, since some measurements are visible

WILLIAM AND MARY LOWBOY

Figure 21

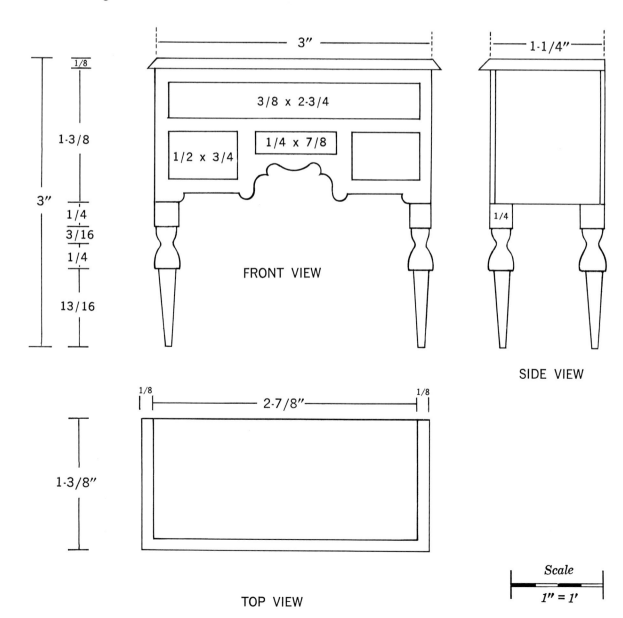

FRONT VIEW

SIDE VIEW

TOP VIEW

Scale

1″ = 1′

Photo 37: Lowboy with William and Mary Legs. Photo: Fred Slater

in one view only. Dimensions seen on more than one view need not be repeated and will keep the pattern uncluttered.

If the legs are highly styled and to be constructed from a separate pattern, it is not necessary to draw more than just a simplified leg of the proper height in developing the views.

The pattern indicates the allowance that must be made in the side view for the thickness of the front and back panels. Cut two pieces from the front view for front and back pieces; or when the front is especially elaborate as in the case of the lowboy, you can cut out a simple rectangle for the hidden back panel. Cut two pieces from the side view to make both side panels. It is desirable to fill in the lower bottom of the case with wood panels to give a completed appearance to the viewer who tips the vignette and looks underneath and, most importantly, to provide a surface on which to fasten the legs.

WOOD OVER CARDBOARD

Many case piece designs, those with boxlike structures, lend themselves to another construction approach in which a sturdy basic form is constructed of illustration board or three or four thicknesses of thin cardboard laminated together. To provide the wood exterior, you veneer thin pieces of wood, either ⅟₁₆″ or ⅟₃₂″ balsa or basswood, to the form. Make the form slightly smaller than the finished overall dimensions to allow for the thickness of the veneered panels.

This method is especially useful for designs with sculptured aprons, since elaborate curves are easier to cut from thin woods and delicacy of line is easier to achieve. The wood-over-cardboard method is illustrated in Photo 38 for the William and Mary lowboy (Photo 37).

The corner cupboard with curved hutch, seen in the music room (Photo 17), shows another method of using wood over cardboard. Balsa wood, ⅟₃₂″ thick with the graining running up and down, was glued onto a curved cardboard form and then stained.

CONTOURED CHESTS

Bombé chests and cabinet pieces with serpentine or contoured lines can be constructed by two methods.

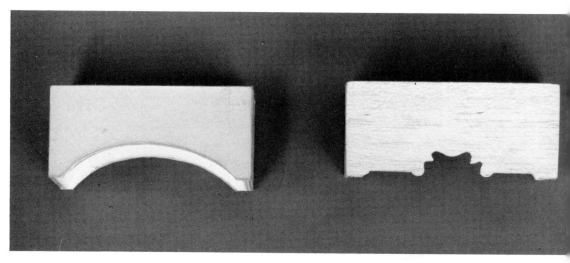

Photo 38: Thin Wood Laminated to Sturdy Cardboard Form. Photo: Fred Slater

Photo 39: Bombé Shape from Solid Balsa Block. Photo: Fred Slater

You may whittle and then sand the desired shape from a solid block of balsa, starting with a piece of wood that measures to the desired height and the widest contour, such as the kettle shape in Photo 39. You can provide drawers and other detailing by scoring them in after the basic shape is obtained, or by adding them with ⅟₃₂″ balsa that is pliable and thin enough to follow the contour when glued on. One disadvantage of the solid block method is the possibility of hitting a pulpy or fibrous area in the wood that results in a flaw or hole. If this occurs, use wood fill to level the surface again. If the piece is to be stained, the wood fill must match the stain. If the piece is to be painted, the sanded down wood fill presents no problem.

In the other method you laminate three or four thin strips of wood onto the basic wood panel (Figure 22) with white glue. Width and thickness of the strips is determined by the degree of contour desired. Shave off the edges of each strip with the craft knife until the basic shape is approximately obtained. The final shaping and smoothness are achieved with vigorous sanding, first with rough sandpaper and then a fine finishing paper. Fill in the open space at the corners when the front and side panels are assembled with a square post of wood

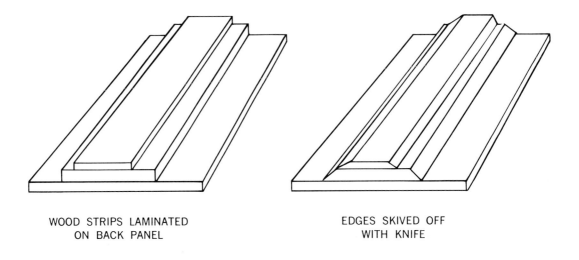

WOOD STRIPS LAMINATED
ON BACK PANEL

EDGES SKIVED OFF
WITH KNIFE

Figure 22

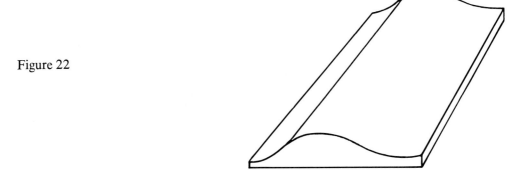

ROUGH SANDED TO FINAL
CONTOURED SHAPE

that can be carved and sanded to the contour or that can be decoratively shaped as an accent to the total design. Drawers made of $\frac{1}{32}''$ wood will follow the contour when glued on or they may be scored in by knife. Take care to do the lamination neatly without any excesses of glue to act as a barrier to stain. The rough sanding that molds the individual strips into a smoothly shaped contour and the addition of drawers and molding make it possible to get a good stained finish (see Victorian style chest in Photo 40). You can also paint the piece and decorate it with paper cutouts or painted designs, if desired.

Photo 40: Victorian Boudoir, Susan Rogers Braun. 6½″ x 8½″ x 2¼″. Photo:
George Peterson

CARDBOARD DESIGNS

Occasionally a cabinet-style piece can be constructed, not of wood, but of illustration board with deceptively realistic results. The body of the American slant top desk (Photo 36) was made entirely of illustration board with only the decorative bandings, the base molding, and the ball feet in wood. You cannot stain cardboard to pass as wood, but in this instance a burled veneer surface was achieved first by sanding the illustration board, wiping it lightly with stain, and then stippling on more stain with a flat-ended brush.

You will find that illustration board construction lends itself extremely well to cabinet pieces that will be painted and further decorated with pasted-on or painted designs.

Another method of cardboard construction is exemplified in the elegant curved console (Photo 41), in which you make the basic form by gluing a half section of the cardboard tubing from a large roll of wrapping paper or gift ribbon to a sturdy cardboard back panel. The illustrated piece has a marble top made of paper glued on a thin piece of cardboard and the floral, fruit, and scroll embellishments are simply a black and white magazine print of a rug which was hand-colored with pencils and glued onto the form. Decorative wood banding, the back rail, feet, and metal hardware were then added. You could decorate similar consoles first by painting and then by adding hand-painted or pasted-on designs.

The hanging cupboard illustrated in Chapter Nine is another example of the achievement of fine little designs from simple pasteboard and paper techniques.

Photo 41: Decorated Console on Cardboard Form, Susan Rogers Braun. Photo: George Peterson

UPHOLSTERED DESIGNS

There are two approaches to the making of upholstered chairs and sofas—one in which you make a rigid, straight line form of cardboard and accomplish the shaping primarily with padding; the other, a technique in which you shape the cardboard form itself in such a manner that only slight padding or no padding at all is required under the covering fabric. Trims and legs are made of wood and attached after upholstering.

Padding in miniature designs should always be held to a minimum to avoid the appearance of overstuffing. You can use cotton, thin foam, or fabric scraps. Upholstering experience on full-size pieces is not a prerequisite, for fabric coverings are glued on and there is no sewing.

To hide "seams" if necessary or desired, glue on decorative welting of tiny cords, or braided flosses and threads. Patterned and striped fabrics should be in proper scale. Avoid fabrics that are thick and bulky.

With the first method, shown in Photo 42 of a Victorian sofa in production, you cut the back and side pieces out of stiff cardboard. Add rounded balsa to the top of the side pieces to create the arm rest. Glue on enough padding to achieve the shaping and then upholster. If the front of the seat is to be curved, glue a shaped piece of balsa to the front edge. Then cover the seat unit with upholstery fabric, pulling it tautly over the front and gluing it to the underside of the seat.

The second method requires the manipulation of thin cardboard to a finished shape with all the contours "built in" and minimal padding or none at all needed. Photo 43 shows a finished loveseat and Photo 44

Photo 42: Victorian Sofa During Production, Using Stiff Form Technique with Padding to Shape. Photo: Fred Slater

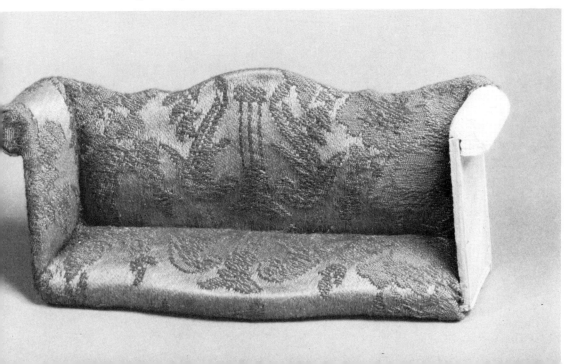

Photo 43: Camelback Loveseat. Photo: Fred Slater

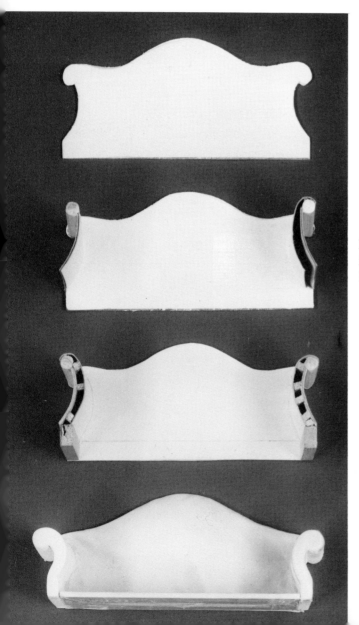

Photo 44: Loveseat Construction Steps Utilizing Contoured Cardboard Form for Shaping. Photo: Fred Slater

illustrates the construction steps that achieve the delicate curves of this loveseat design.

Make the camel (or hump) back from two laminated thin pieces of cardboard. Start the curved arm construction with a ¼″ rounded piece of balsa glued and pinned to the back piece. Force thin cardboard pieces into the desired curve of both the inside and outside of the arm, gluing them to the back and holding until dry. Leave a shaped channel into which scraps of balsa can be glued to reinforce the shaping and strengthen the arm. Glue in balsa pieces to complete the lower arm. Cut a separate piece of cardboard to cover the front of each arm and glue into place. At this point extra rigidity of the whole design can be provided by applying one or two coats of paint or gesso. A 1″ scale pattern of the back, side pieces, and legs of this loveseat are given in Figure 23.

Upholster the back first, adding only a slight suggestion of padding in the center. Cover the front of the armrests next, clipping and overlapping the fabric onto the sides. The remainder of the arm is then covered with a folded piece of fabric in which the fold actually gives the appearance of tiny welting. Cover the seat unit separately and glue it into place. The seat cushion is made by covering wood or thick cardboard with two or three loose layers of fabric to give a soft, filled look. You do not need to add padding for shaping on the basic form except for the small amount on the seat back.

Since only the front and sides of a chair or sofa are likely to be seen in a vignette, it is not necessary to cover the back, although you may finish it by covering a thin cardboard of the proper shape with the selected fabric and then gluing it in place.

The Sheraton-style tub chair (Photo 45) is another example of the use of laminated thin cardboard to make the basic modeled form.

Glue together two pieces of thin cardboard cut from the pattern part that represents the chair body and side arms (Figure 24). Cut one slightly wider to accommodate curving around the inside piece. Immediately after gluing them, hold them firmly around a jar, glass, or can measuring 2″ in diameter for 10 to 15 minutes while glue is drying. Trim the front of the arms to eliminate any overhanging edge. The inside bottom edge of the form should be traced to make an exact pattern for the seat cushion. The development of steps is shown in Photo 46.

Glue a slight amount of padding to the inside of the chair, starting with none in the seat area and tapering gently upward to the back and

CAMELBACK LOVESEAT

Figure 23

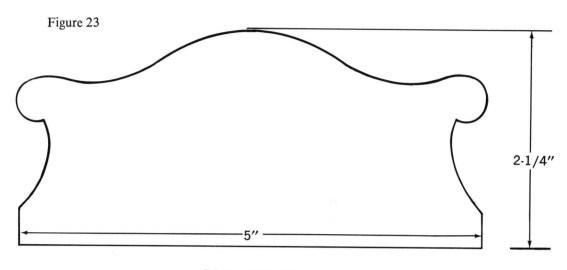

BACK PATTERN

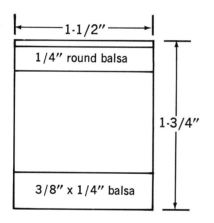

SIDE VIEW OF
ARM CONSTRUCTION

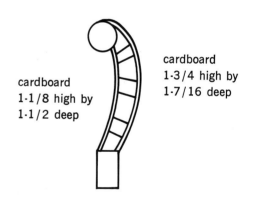

FRONT VIEW OF
ARM CONSTRUCTION

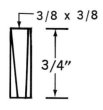

LEG
PATTERN

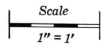

SEAT AND CUSHION PIECES
ARE 4-1/2″ wide by 1-3/8″ deep

Photo 45: Tub Chair in Sheraton Style.
Photo: Fred Slater

upper arms. Cut the fabric to upholster the inside of the chair from the original pattern, slightly enlarged by an allowance to overlap to the reverse side. Glue it first to the inner base of the chair and draw it tightly up to and over the top, clipping every ½ " at the top to permit smooth gluing to the outside of the chair form. Such clipping should not be so deep that it is visible along the top edge of the chair after gluing.

Cut the fabric for the outside of the chair about ¼ " larger than the original pattern. Shape it to fit exactly on the outside of the chair by turning the excess in with an iron or finger pressing. Depending upon the fabric used and the quality of workmanship, the top "seam" need not always be covered but, if desired, it can be hidden under tiny welting.

Cut the seat out of ¼ " balsa from the pattern that was made after

TUB CHAIR

Reproduction in Sheraton style

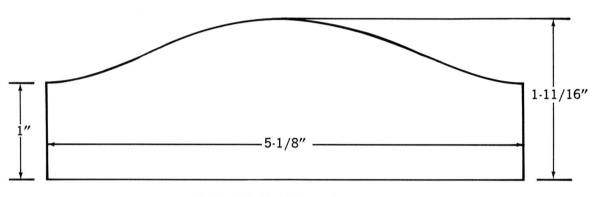

1"

5-1/8"

1-11/16"

CHAIR BODY AND SIDE ARMS

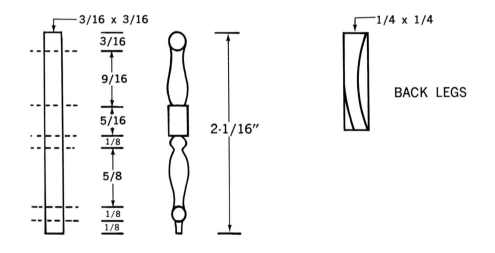

3/16 x 3/16

3/16

9/16

5/16

1/8

5/8

1/8

1/8

2-1/16"

1/4 x 1/4

BACK LEGS

FRONT LEGS

Figure 24

Scale

1" = 1'

Photo 46: Tub Chair Development Steps. Photo: Fred Slater

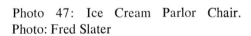

Photo 47: Ice Cream Parlor Chair.
Photo: Fred Slater

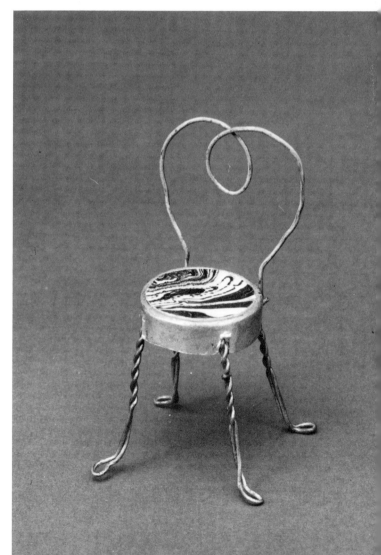

the chair form was molded. Cover it with fabric and glue into place. Glue in legs (Figure 24) made of wood. For added strength, you can insert sequin pins, with heads cut off, into the legs and chair seat.

ICE CREAM PARLOR CHAIR

You can improvise an ice cream parlor chair (Photo 47) in 1″ scale using the twisted wire cage atop some champagne bottles. Cut off the excess wire around the base, leaving attached just enough to make the looped foot of the one incomplete leg. Use a pliers to shape it. Form the back from pliable thick-gauge wire, bending and looping it into a pretzel, heart, or other design, and fasten the ends to the upper rear legs. Make a round collar from a strip of ¼″-wide laminated cardboard, notching it to fit over the legs. This collar holds the back in position and serves as the frame of the seat. Finish the seat with a wood, cardboard, or cushion insert.

OTHER PATTERNS

Following are three selected designs (Photos 48, 49, and 50) with their basic pattern parts—a trestle table (Figure 25), ladderback chair (Figure 26), and slant top desk (Figure 27). All are in 1″ scale. The needed dimensions are found by reading all views.

Photo 48: Trestle Table. Photo: Fred Slater

Photo 49: Ladderback Chair. Photo: Fred Slater

Photo 50: American Slant Top Desk. Photo: Fred Slater

TRESTLE TABLE

Figure 25

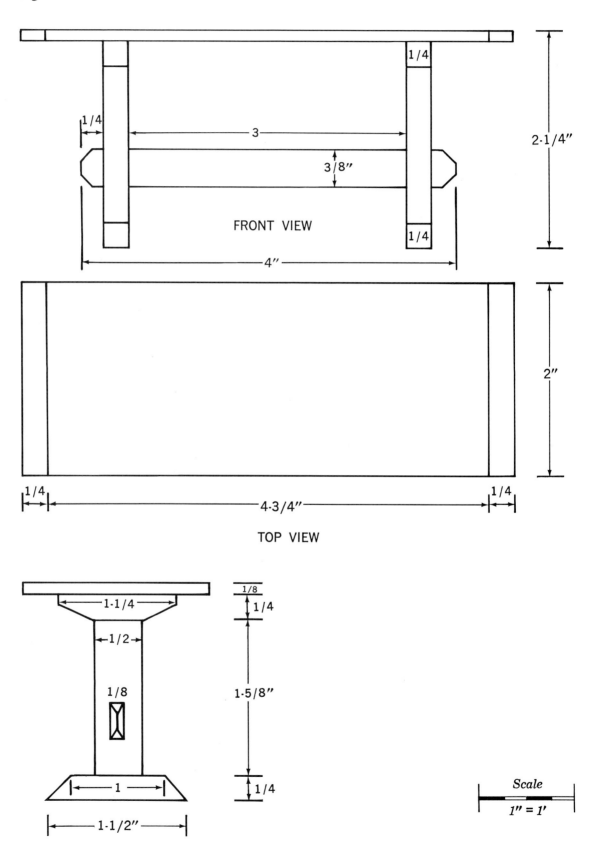

FRONT VIEW

TOP VIEW

END VIEW

Scale
1″ = 1′

LADDERBACK CHAIR

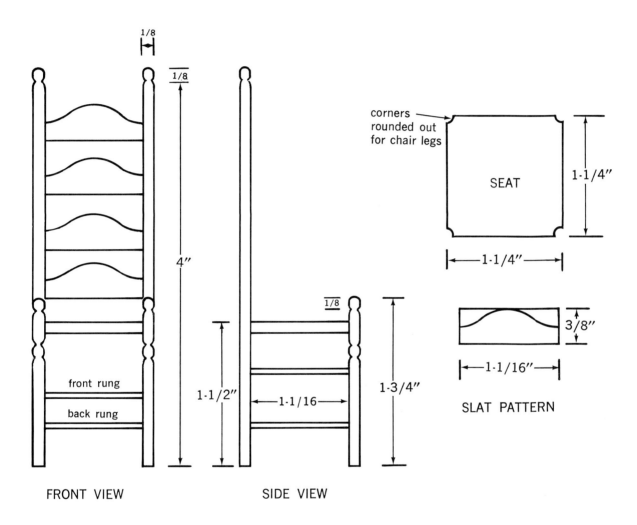

corners
rounded out
for chair legs

SEAT

1-1/4"

1-1/4"

3/8"

1-1/16"

SLAT PATTERN

1/8

1/8

4"

front rung

back rung

1-1/2"

1-1/16

1/8

1-3/4"

FRONT VIEW

SIDE VIEW

Figure 26

Scale
1" = 1'

Figure 27   AMERICAN
                                SLANT TOP DESK

                            (circa 1700, burled
                             finish, ball feet)

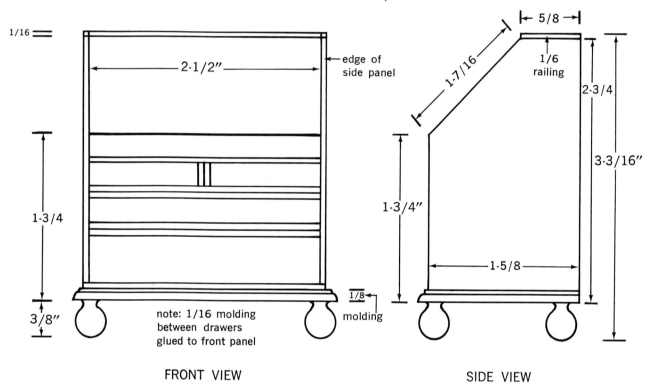

FRONT VIEW   SIDE VIEW

note: 1/16 molding
between drawers
glued to front panel

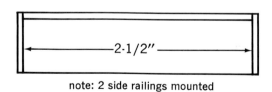

note: 2 side railings mounted
on top of side panels

TOP VIEW
(partial)

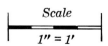

Scale

1" = 1'

Index